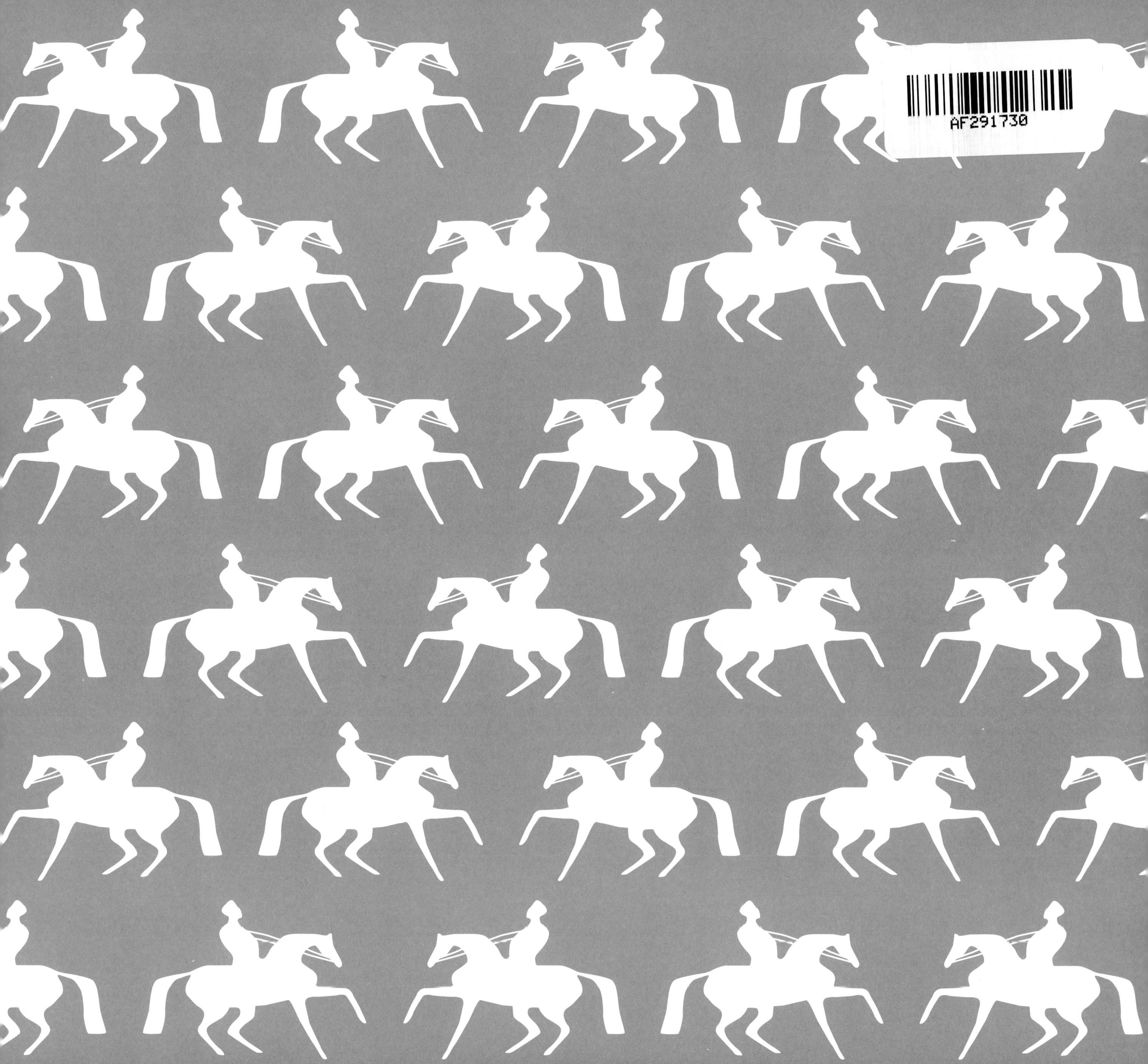

AF291730

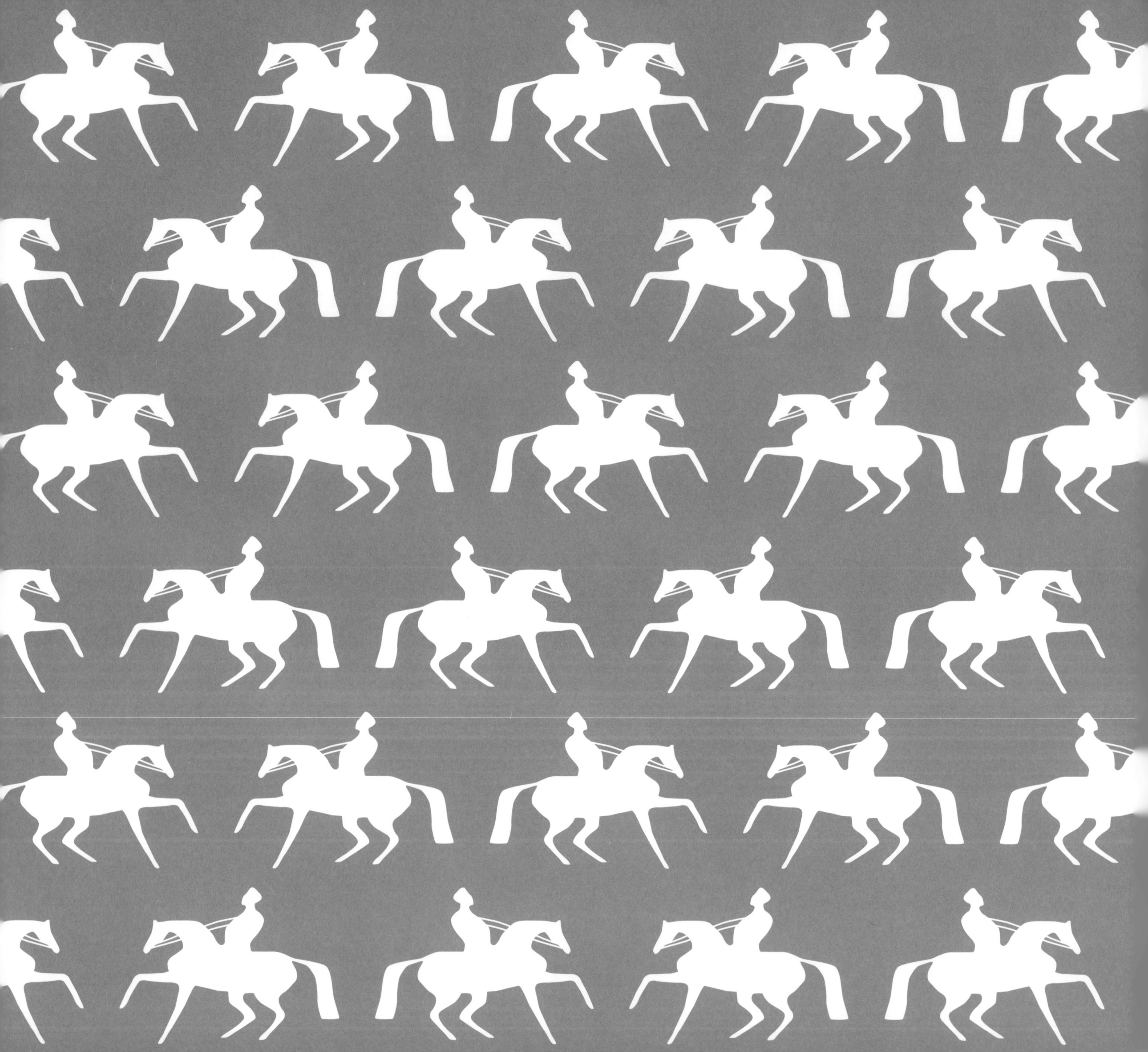

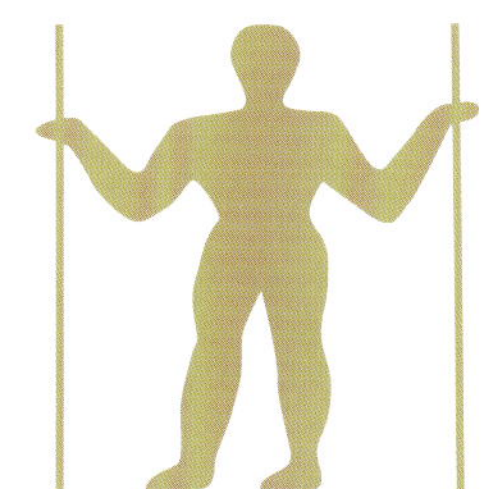

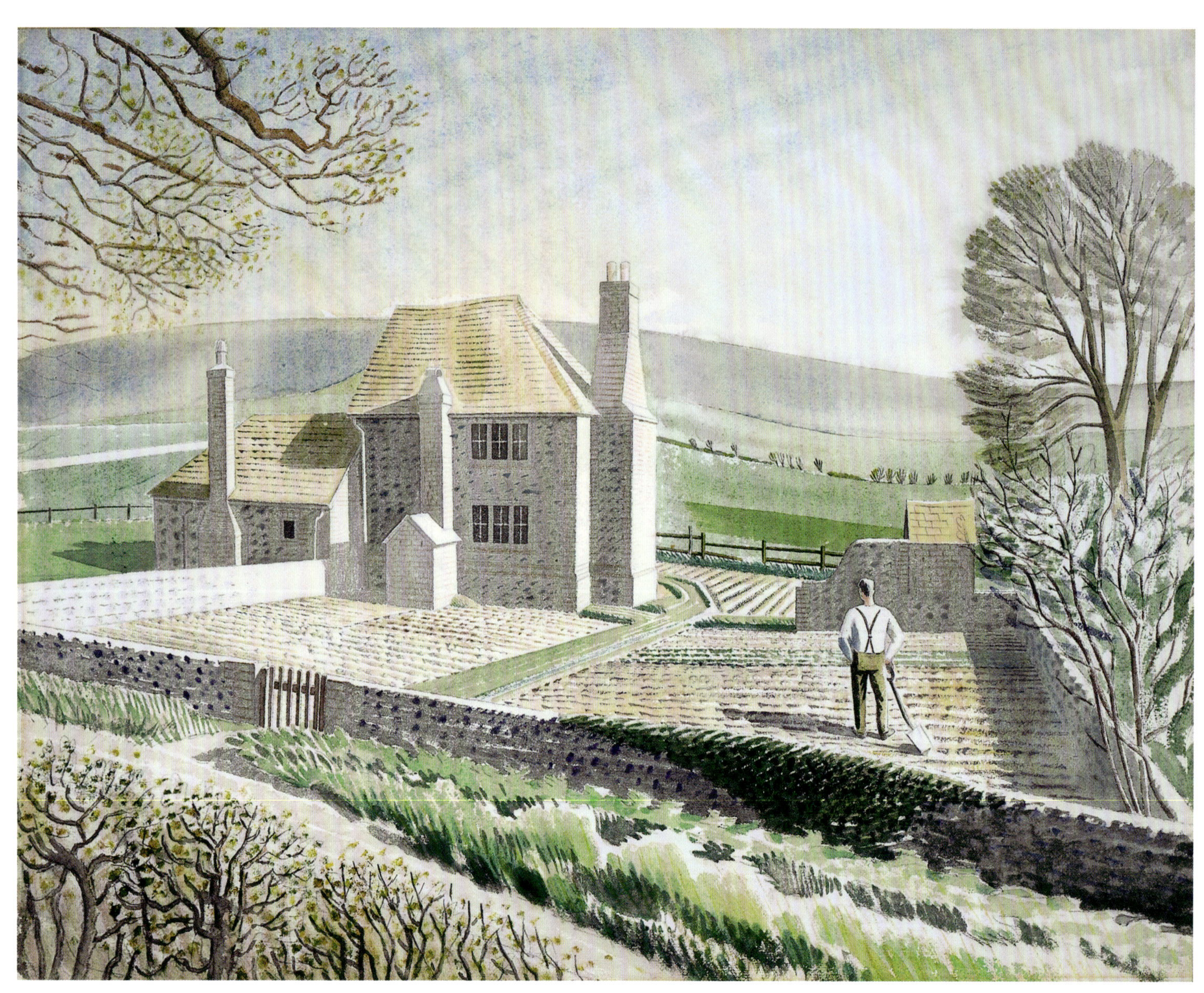

Shepherd's Cottage (The Lay), 1934, watercolour, 44.5 x 56.6 cm, private collection.

James Russell

RAVILIOUS IN PICTURES
SUSSEX AND THE DOWNS

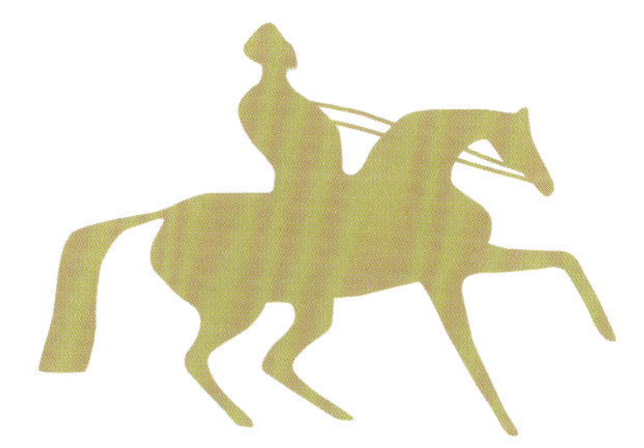

The Mainstone Press

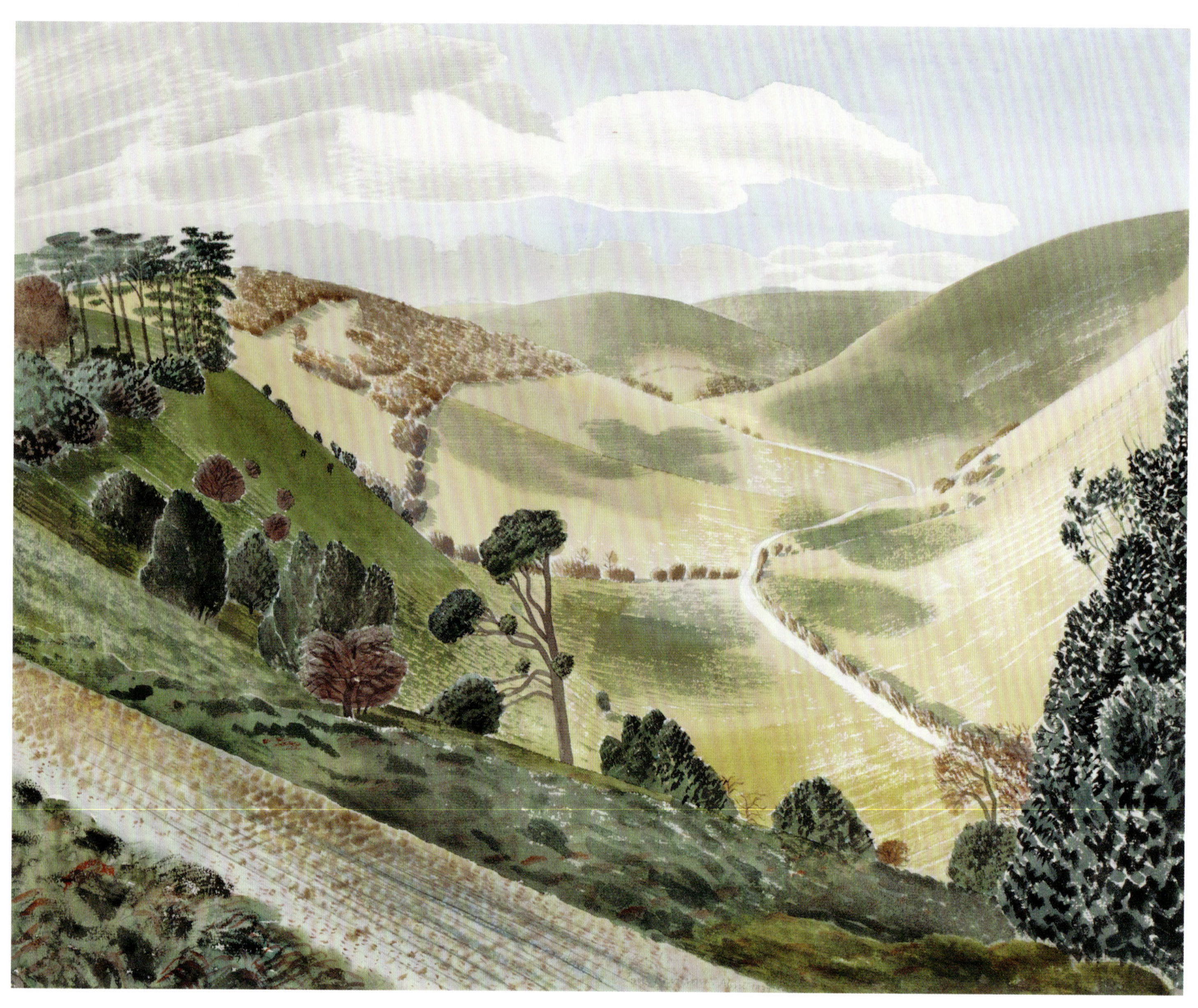

The Causeway, Wiltshire Downs, 1937, watercolour, 44.5 x 54.6 cm, Victoria and Albert Museum, London.

INTRODUCTION

The landscape that most inspired Eric Ravilious was, by his own admission, the chalk Downland of southern England. Born in Acton in 1903, he moved to Eastbourne as a boy and returned to teach there after graduating from the Royal College of Art in 1925. But although paintings from this period hint at the artist Ravilious would become, it was his rediscovery of the Sussex Downs when in his early thirties that proved crucial. From 1934, when he visited artist and designer Peggy Angus at her cottage below Beddingham Hill, until his appointment as a war artist in December 1939, he created a remarkable body of work that ranges geographically across Sussex, Wiltshire, Oxfordshire and Dorset, and in subject from ancient chalk figures to a 20th-century cement works.

In his lifetime Ravilious was known by fellow painters as the artist who sold all his paintings, but after his death in 1942, while on active service as a war artist, his legacy was not fully appreciated for many years. Recently, interest in his work has blossomed, however, and it is intriguing that this renaissance should have come at a time when the English landscape and its customs and culture are also the subject of renewed enthusiasm. In this book, the first in the series of *Ravilious in Pictures*, we aim to explore both the artist's work and the landscape that inspired him, and in the following pages you will find a selection of watercolours, each accompanied by a short essay that investigates place, character and time. These essays focus on the everyday lives of Ravilious and the people around him, on English culture in the 1930s, and on the history of the landscape that the artist studied and portrayed.

Though Ravilious made very little public comment about his work, he left a fascinating body of private correspondence, much of which has now been edited by his daughter, Anne Ullmann, and published by the Fleece Press. Drawing on these letters and other sources we can offer an intimate portrait of the artist at work, perching on a clifftop to sketch the Beachy Head lighthouse or snagging his trousers on a barbed-wire fence as he rushes off to start work on the Cerne Abbas giant. In spirit, our approach resembles that adopted by John Betjeman as editor of the *Shell Guides* in the 1930s, which Candida Lycett Green recently summarised as 'human reactions to places, rather than academic reactions'.

There is an intriguing parallel between Betjeman's guidebooks and the watercolours painted by Ravilious. Both editor and artist were fascinated by the English landscape, and both revived a long-established genre. In the 18th century a vogue for travel created demand for guidebooks and also for images of notable sights. Being ideal both for work outside the studio and for copying onto the etching plate, watercolour emerged as the medium of choice for Francis Towne and other topographical painters. Towne was rediscovered at the turn of the 20th century and became — along with John Sell Cotman and Samuel Palmer — a source of inspiration for Ravilious when he studied at the Royal College of Art in the early 1920s.

When he graduated in 1925 travel was again coming into fashion, as increasing numbers of people began exploring Britain by car and bus. A new generation of topographical writers, notably H. V. Morton and Thomas Burke, catered to the metropolitan traveller, while Shell sponsored guidebooks and commissioned landscape paintings to advertise its petrol.

With his drawing board in a canvas satchel and a lightweight sketching easel on his shoulder, Ravilious explored the Downs like the topographical painters of old, either on foot or, when someone could be persuaded to act as chauffeur, by car. Naturally drawn to the distinctive and particular, he continually sought subjects that no one had painted before. In a light-hearted letter of November 1937, John Nash's wife Christine responded to his request for ideas by recommending a trip to Dorset. 'Reference to the "Shell Guide to Dorset" by Paul Nash will give you some idea of the strangeness of the Country…' she wrote, continuing: 'If you should prefer something brown-yellower, and with no trees at all, we would suggest the Sand-Dunes called Braunton Barrows in N. Devon… We believe this is practically Virgin Soil as regards the Painter's Activities.'

Over the next eighteen months Ravilious travelled as far as Capel-y-ffin in Wales and to the French port of Le Havre, but in 1939 he returned to the Downs once again, only with a different approach. Instead of seeking out new sights, he chose well-known subjects like the Long Man of Wilmington and painted them from unexpected angles or in unusual ways to bring them to life. In this he was ahead of his time, anticipating the enthusiastic rediscovery of the local and distinctive inspired by Sue Clifford and Angela King of landscape charity Common Ground. In their recent book *England in Particular*, Clifford and King celebrate 'the extraordinary richness of our everyday surroundings', while offering 'a way of looking that has universal potential, but is best done on an intimate scale'. It is at the level of field or street, after all, that life is lived.

The loudest challenge to this view was issued by Rudyard Kipling, who asked, 'What do they know of England that only England know?' G. K. Chesterton gave, in his 1905 book *Heretics*, a compelling answer: 'The man in the saloon steamer has seen all the races of men, and he is thinking of the things that divide men – diet, dress, decorum … The man in the cabbage field has seen nothing at all; but he is thinking of the things that unite men – hunger and babies, and the beauty of women, and the promise or menace of the sky.'

Until he became a war artist Eric Ravilious rarely left England, but he well appreciated both the things that unite men and the extraordinary richness of his surroundings. Wherever he chose to focus – on the interior of a railway compartment, or a farm roller, or a figure carved into a hillside – he brought his subject to life in a way that made contemporary critics reach for words like 'mystical' and 'magical'. Enchanted equally by teapots and lighthouses, chalk giants and greenhouses, Ravilious has left us with a captivating portrait of Sussex and the Downs that combines a topographer's eye for detail with a seer's extraordinary vision.

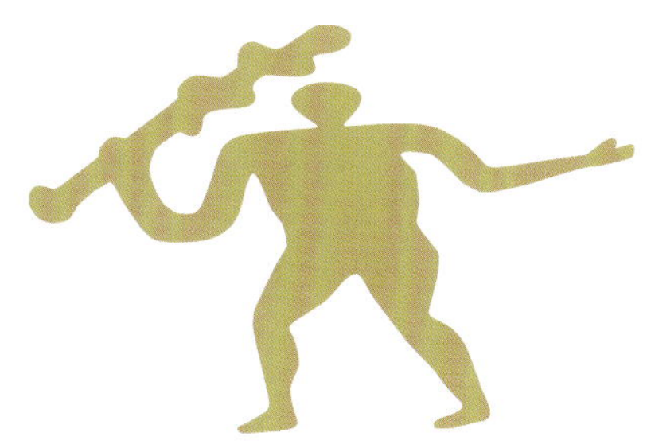

THE PAINTINGS

FIRLE BEACON

Beyond the fence, beneath dramatic clouds, Firle Beacon rises. In 1927 Eric Ravilious had recently graduated from the Royal College of Art and was teaching at the Eastbourne School of Art, his alma mater. He liked to take students out by bicycle or bus on sketching expeditions to nearby villages: Wilmington, Alfriston and other Saxon outposts at the south-eastern tip of Downland.

Fast gaining renown as a wood engraver, the artist confessed to students his desire to revive the English tradition of watercolour painting, and here we see both his first depiction of the South Downs and early hints of the artist he would become. The fence dividing us from the countryside beyond is meticulously rendered, while the gaps where slats are missing insist that this is a specific section of a particular fence.

An intense focus on place and object would become a hallmark of the artist's work, and as a teacher he encouraged students not only to look and sketch, but also to read widely. He loved the great chroniclers of the English countryside, writers like W. H. Hudson, Richard Jefferies and Edward Thomas, but above all he admired Gilbert White, the 18th-century naturalist who immortalised the Hampshire village of Selborne, and who wrote: 'Though I have now travelled the Sussex-downs upwards of thirty years, yet I still investigate that chain of majestic mountains with fresh admiration year by year, and I think I see new beauties every time I traverse it…'

Stretching from Eastbourne to Winchester, these southern hills form part of England's skeleton, the great limbs of chalk that extend west into Dorset and Wiltshire and north into Buckinghamshire. Firle Beacon is one of White's majestic mountains, its summit, topped by a long barrow, dominating the countryside between Eastbourne and Lewes. Beneath this peak, the country over which Ravilious looked in the summer of 1927 had its landowners, tenants, farmers and shepherds. Below the Beacon, the village of West Firle was the domain of the Gage family, owners of the Firle Estate, while the land to the north belonged to the 800-year-old Glynde Estate.

Though Ravilious had moved to Eastbourne as a boy, he did not know the landscape around Firle Beacon, and it would be some time before he discovered it. He would soon marry his most talented student, Eastbourne native Tirzah Garwood, but the trajectory of his career would take him away from the South Downs, to London and then Essex. Indeed, seven years would pass before his old friend Peggy Angus brought him to a shepherd's cottage, in the heart of this ancient countryside.

Firle Beacon, Sussex, 1927, watercolour, 40.0 x 49.5 cm, National Museums & Galleries of Wales.

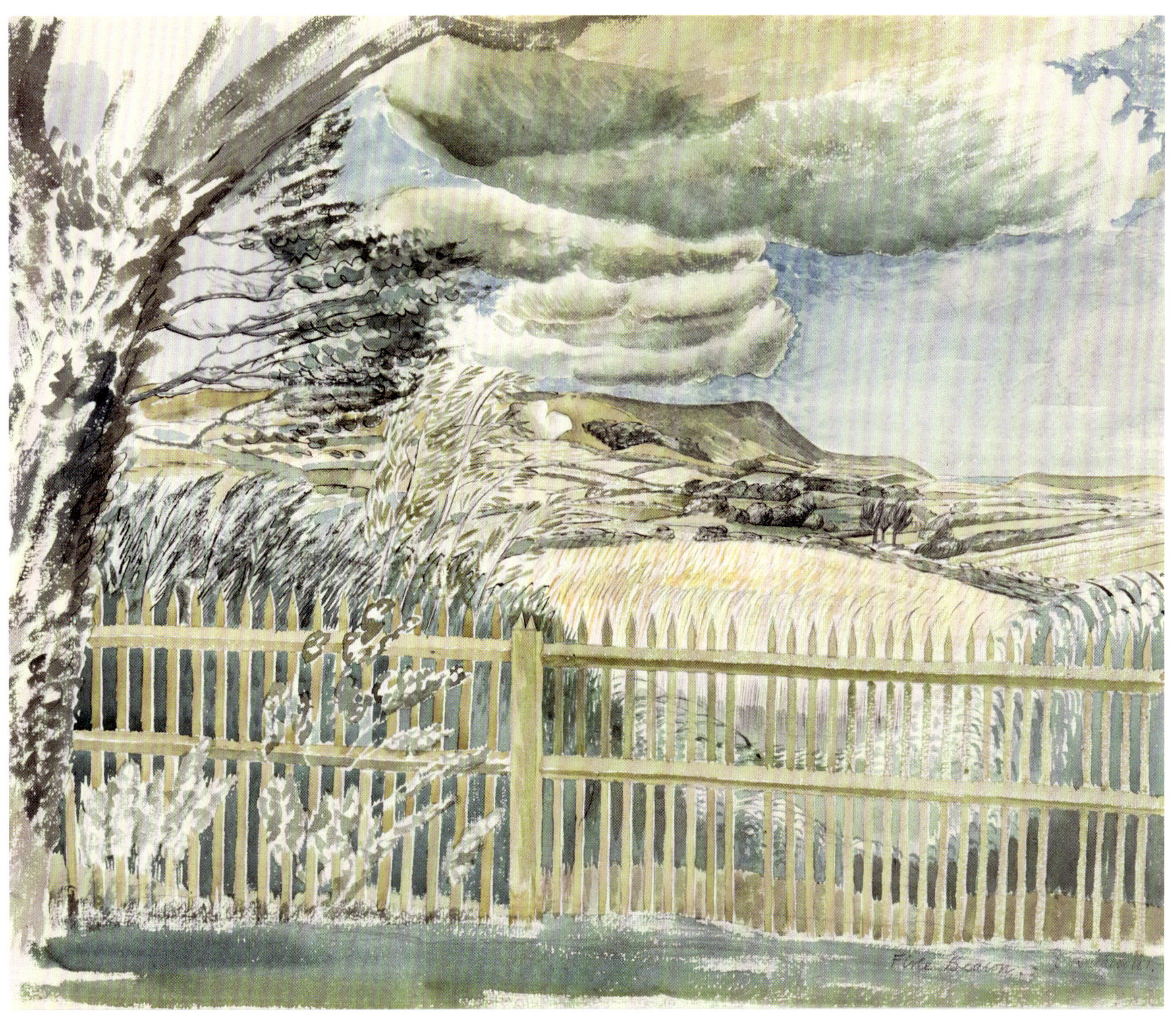

FURLONGS

In the spring of 1934 Ravilious returned to the South Downs, staying at the cottage shown here. In the background a chalk lane leads to Beddingham Hill – Firle Beacon is out of sight to the left – while horse-drawn carts deliver hay below. Today the horses and haystacks are gone, but the cottage remains. If you walk from Charleston Farmhouse, that famous Sussex outpost of Bloomsbury, via the village of Firle to Virginia Woolf's house at Rodmell, you pass right by 'The Furlongs', as the Ordnance Survey map calls it. But you would never know that this stark flint-faced cottage had once been the home of designer Peggy Angus and the matrix of much strange and inventive creation.

She found the cottage in 1933, when house-hunting on foot along the Downs, and fell in love with it at once. But although the place was empty, the front door locked and enmeshed in ivy, its owner, tenant farmer Dick Freeman, was reluctant to let it to her. A woman of determined character, Angus camped outside, enduring wind and weather, until he relented. Angus had studied at the RCA with Bawden and Ravilious and that autumn she visited them in Essex; the following spring Eric and his wife Tirzah returned the visit – the first names on a Furlongs guest list that would include Helen Binyon, Edward and Charlotte Bawden, Percy Horton, Maurice de Saumarez, John and Myfanwy Piper, Olive Cook and Edwin Smith, not to mention Eric and Tirzah's children and their families. Built for the shepherds of the Glynde Estate, whose flocks roamed the hills above, the house became a retreat for artists and a base for their explorations of the surrounding country.

Not everyone admired this Bohemian settlement. Colonel Garwood, Tirzah's conservative father, disapproved of Peggy's communist ideals and referred to her as the Red Angus. 'An evasive letter from Tirzah,' he once noted in his diary, 'who is staying with a Bolshie woman and does not wish to be visited.'

The appearance of a car in the lane was likely to send people scurrying into the hills. Generally guests travelled by train to Glynde station, disembarked with rucksacks and painting gear, and headed south through the village, passing the Trevor Arms and the row of cottages – Spring Gardens – where Mrs Soames the laundress lived. On the far side of the Lewes–Eastbourne road a leafy lane led uphill to an open field, with the swelling slopes of the chalk Downs beyond, their rounded tops bare against the sky. Here, visitors turned right along a track to the cottage, as you can still today. Outwardly Furlongs appears little changed, with the same flint wall enclosing an emerald lawn.

Furlongs, 1934, watercolour, 43.2 x 50.8 cm, private collection.

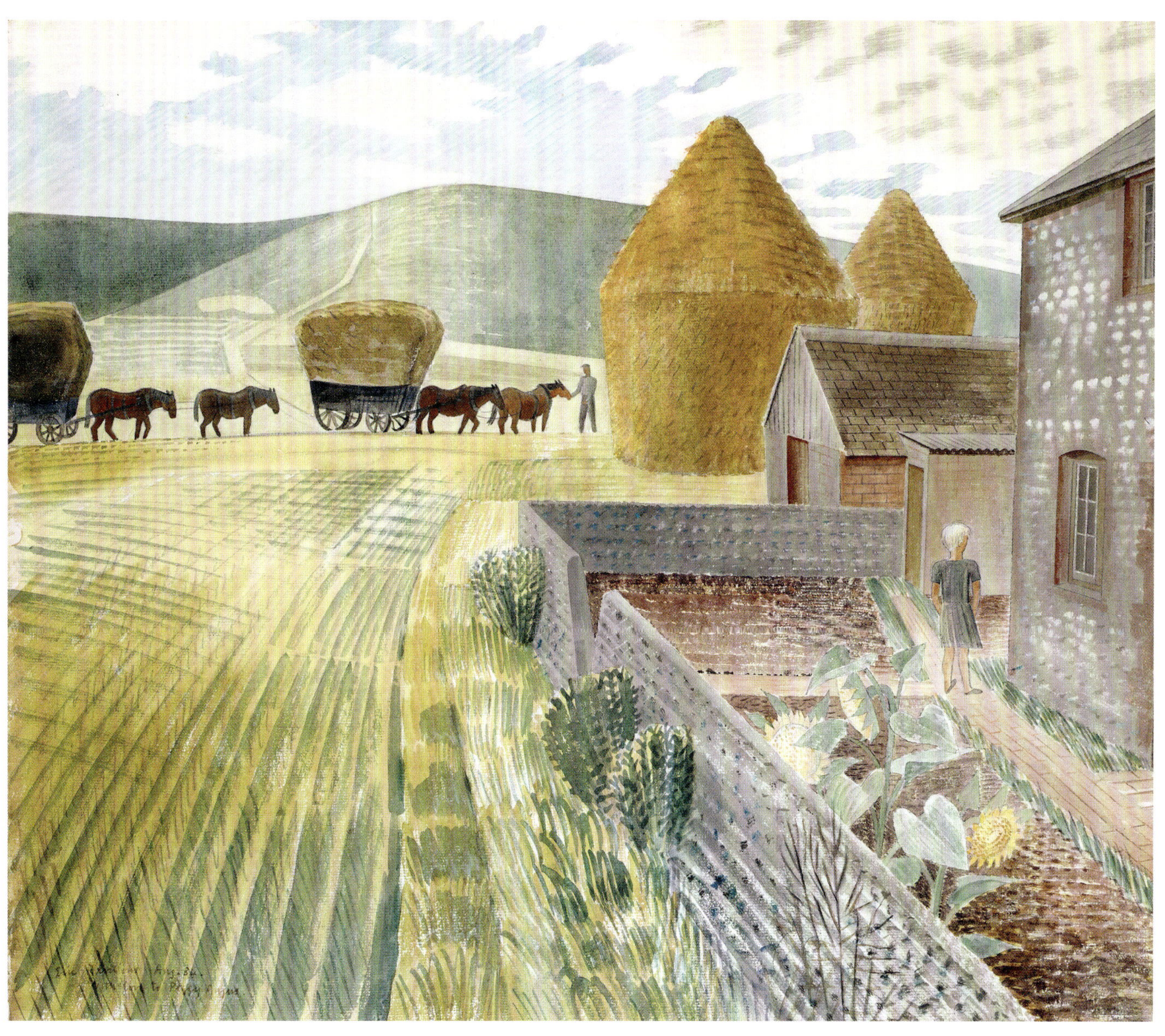

INTERIOR AT FURLONGS

The soft bright light of the Downs floods through an open door into a room that could hardly be plainer. The brick floor is uncovered, the walls undecorated, but red curtains hang at the window and the brightness of the countryside beyond fills the room with life. An overcoat hanging behind the open door and a bentwood chair in front of the window lend the painting a mysterious, even dreamlike quality, but they also reflect the simplicity of life at Furlongs. Water had to be hauled from a well and there was no electricity. Catering arrangements too were fairly basic: 'I am eating my way through a ham,' Ravilious wrote to Peggy Angus in June 1934, 'very good to begin with, getting now a little tough. Mrs Barnes [from the neighbouring cottage] ... now and again brings me in scraps that fall from the Barnes's table – gooseberry pie and what-not.'

Raised in a society that still clung to Victorian codes of behaviour, Ravilious enjoyed both this simplicity and the informality of life at Furlongs, the lack of carpets to object to muddy boots and the picnic meals. Yet the interior of the house was anything but austere. On her second visit Tirzah Ravilious brought marbling apparatus and sheets of Michallet paper, and set about making colourful patterned wallpaper. Her husband, who had been raised in the art of 'junking' at his father's Eastbourne antique shop and was renowned for his ability to find people strange, decorative gifts, led expeditions to junk shops in Lewes.

Before long the cottage was filled with treasures, like the bird cage and rocking chair Ravilious portrayed on the Wedgwood 'Alphabet' mug of 1937, and a large, square-cornered Victorian mirror that fitted neatly into the recess beside the kitchen range. Paintings by Angus and her guests hung on the walls, with the Ravilious watercolour 'Furlongs' over the mantelpiece, illuminated at night by a ruby glass oil lamp – another of Eric's presents. With a fire of sticks and branches gathered from the woods, the small sitting room became a cosy retreat after a day of outdoor painting in springtime.

In summer, with the constant coming and going of exuberant personalities, evenings at Furlongs were often festive occasions, with singing by candlelight around an old harmonium. Angus, Ravilious and Percy Horton had between them a wide repertoire of folk songs and Elizabethan rounds, such as 'Slaves to the world shall be tossed in a blanket' and 'Wind gentle evergreen to form a shade / Around the tomb where Sophocles is laid.'

Even in this stripped-down portrait of the cottage, the energy of the place and its occupants shines through, with those red curtains, tied with bows at the waist, dancing at the window.

Interior at Furlongs, 1939, watercolour, 45.8 x 54.4 cm, private collection, on loan to the Towner Art Gallery, Eastbourne.

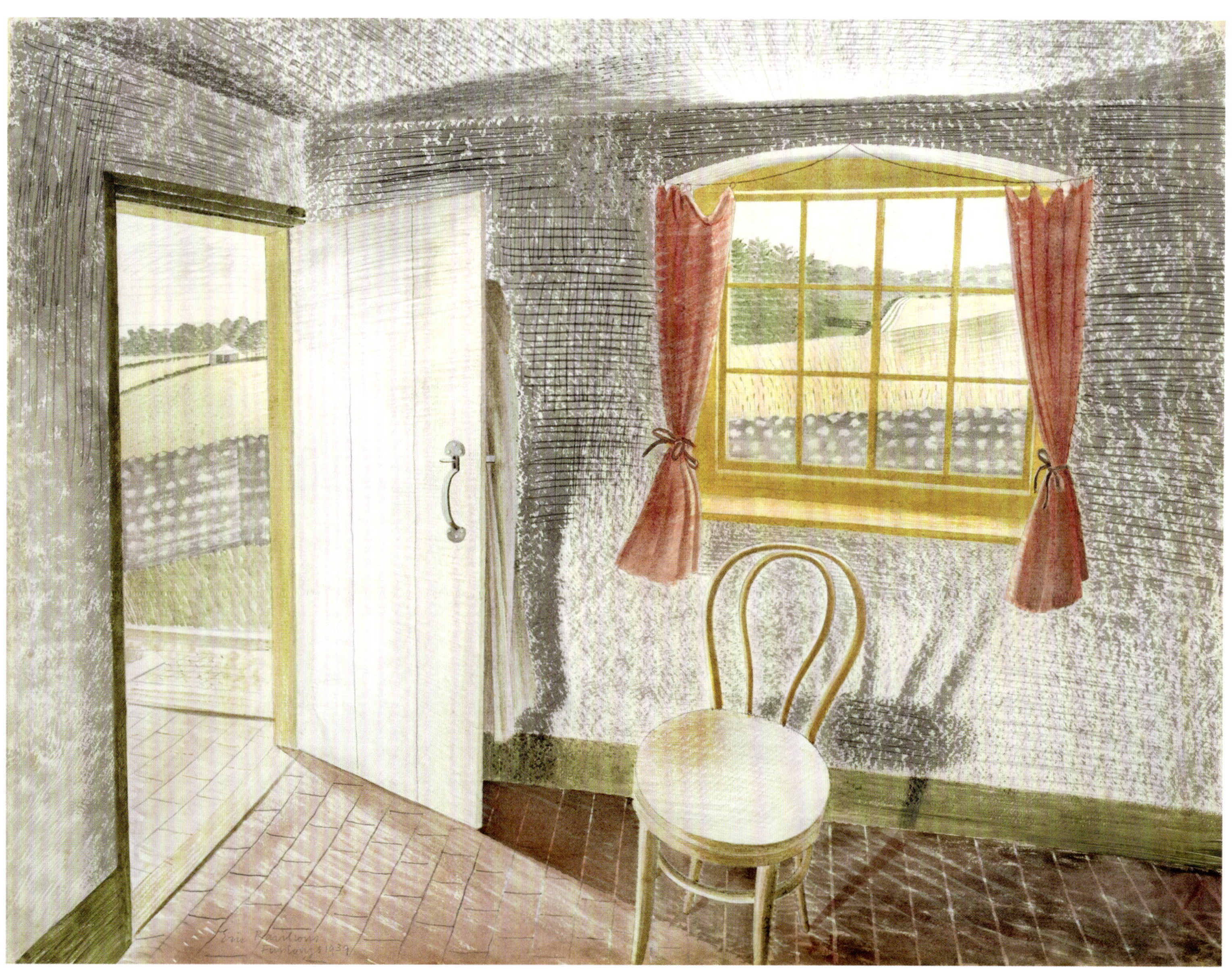

WATERWHEEL

When visitors approached Furlongs from Glynde they crossed the Lewes–Eastbourne road, walked up a tree-lined lane and then turned right past a copse, over which towered the wheel of a creaking wind pump that bore on its vane the mysterious word 'DANDO'.

This wind pump was used to draw water for Little Dene, the grand house you pass as you walk up the lane. With no mains water supply, each cottage or house had its own well, from which residents had to draw their water. So a wind pump was a luxurious labour-saving device; it was also the kind of machine or feature Ravilious loved, and he sketched it right away.

In this painting, a different wind pump stands like a sentinel on the very edge of the cultivated land bordering the Downs, where it also helps to balance a composition of which Ravilious was particularly proud. In general the artist was so self-critical that he tore up three out of every four watercolours he attempted, but he considered this painting a success. The colours used are limited, but cleverly worked to convey the irregular structure of the land, and its dry chalky texture.

In fact chalk holds moisture well, but above the spring line, on the hilltops, drought can be a serious problem, and ingenious methods were used in the past to capture water for sheep and other livestock – and, incidentally, for linnets, finches, hares and badgers. Evidence of such hydrological invention can be seen on the hilltop above Furlongs, in the form of two shallow depressions described on the Ordnance Survey map as 'White Lion Pond' and 'Red Lion Pond'.

These are dewponds, dug and lined with puddled mud to capture not dew so much as rain from summer storms. Until the 1930s they were maintained for the Glynde Estate by a local family, the Wellers, but with improvements in the mains water supply the dewponds fell into disuse. Post-war Peggy Angus gave them a new role, as the setting for spectacular Midsummer Eve bonfire parties. With a good supply of homemade elderflower champagne, she would lead the singing of folk songs and rounds, while potatoes roasted in the fire. One year John Ravilious, the artist's eldest son, released a large homemade fire balloon.

Intended to store water, the ponds became the scene of fire ceremonies. But what of the pump shown in this painting? Given the remote location, Glynde historian Andrew Lusted suggests that Ravilious imported it from elsewhere, to complement the rolling hills. As for the 'DANDO' pump, its remains are still there at the corner of the lane leading to Furlongs, hidden in the dense vegetation.

Waterwheel (South Downs), 1934, watercolour, 45.7 x 55.8 cm, private collection.

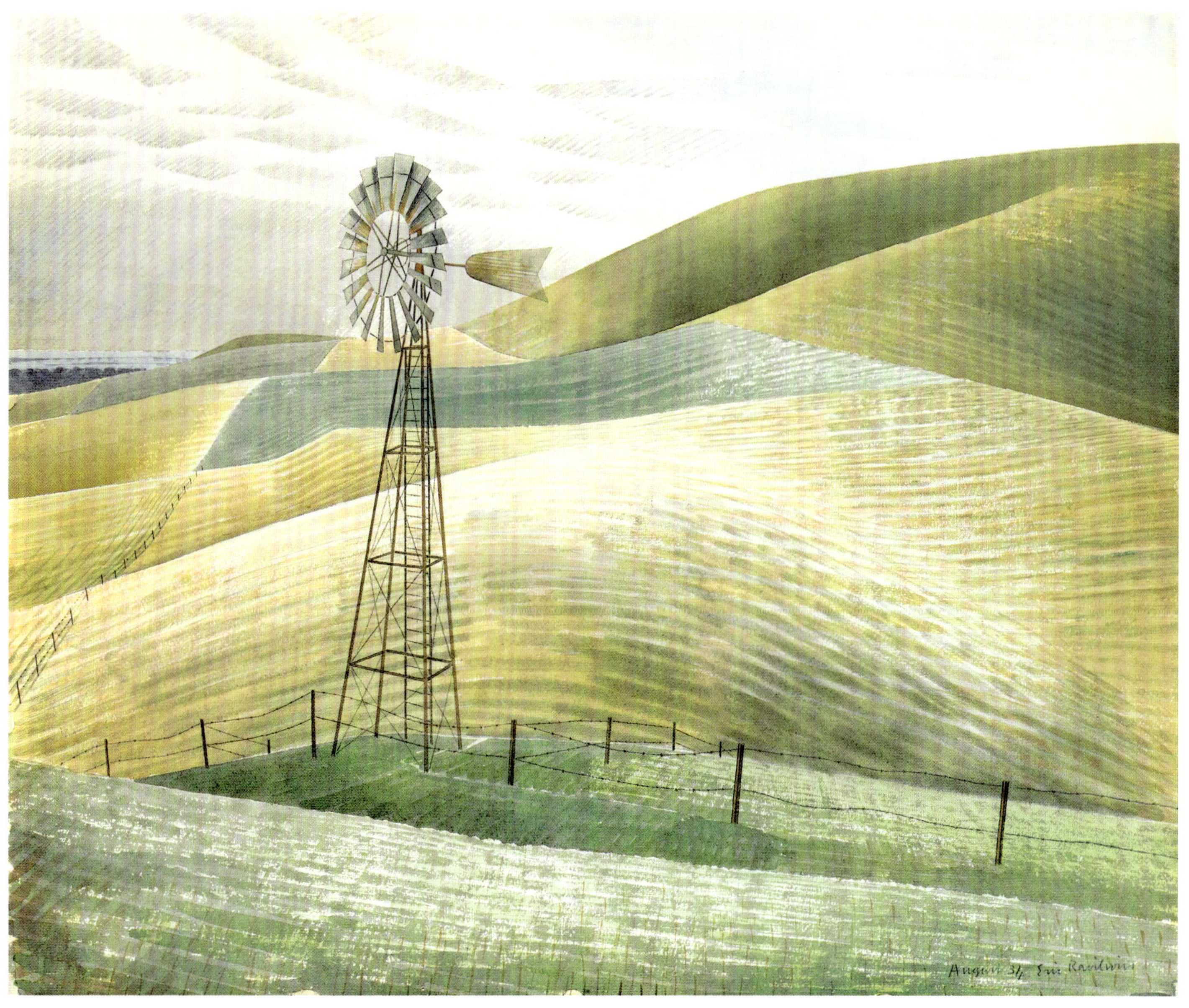

August 34 Eric Ravilious

DOWNS IN WINTER

A field roller stands on the edge of a bleak expanse of land, earth that has been laid bare by the season and the plough. It seems impossible that anything could live or grow here, yet the mood of the painting is not grim. This image of Downland in winter may be austere, and haunting, but it is beautiful too. The sun, not long risen, is low and haloed by clouds. Its soft light brings out the pallor of the land. This is winter in a northern latitude, winter as the still point between the end of one year and the beginning of the next.

The cycle of the seasons recurs frequently as a theme in Ravilious's work, and at Peggy Angus's cottage he painted seedtime ('Mount Caburn') and harvest ('Furlongs'), as well as this vision of Beddingham Hill in winter. Walk along the track from Firle towards the cottage on a clear winter morning and you will see much the same view, but for the TV masts on the summit of the hill – an addition Ravilious might have enjoyed.

Here the hill seems ancient and unchanging, recalling H. J. Massingham's description of the Downs as a 'wild and inspiriting land, whose gates are a ticket-of-leave from Progress and an introduction to the simpler and deeper emotions of our being'. A friend of Ravilious's and a respected and prolific chronicler of the countryside between the wars, Massingham wrote two influential books on English Downland and the civilisation that built its long barrows and hill forts. On his frequent walks he noted the emptiness and solitude of the hilltops in contrast to the mechanical rush of cars in the roads below. The road belongs to us, he writes, the Downs to the dead.

Ravilious captures the deep age and loneliness of the landscape, but in reality the country he saw every day was constantly evolving and rarely empty. Since Medieval times the South Downs had been grazed, then ploughed, then grazed once more during the long Victorian agricultural recession, only to be ploughed again when grain became profitable during and after World War I. The horse-drawn roller standing in the foreground may appear to the modern eye a beautifully crafted antique – its delicate curving shafts perhaps hinting at an even older world of hunters and horned prey – but this was first and foremost an agricultural tool, used in all weathers by the ploughman and his team to prepare the winter earth for sowing.

'You can hardly see country at all from the windows,' Ravilious wrote during one horrendous winter storm. 'Barnes can just be seen with the roller – he has sacks tied round with string so looks much larger than usual. He looks pretty miserable.'

Downs in Winter, 1934, watercolour, 44.5 x 55.5 cm, Towner Art Gallery, Eastbourne.

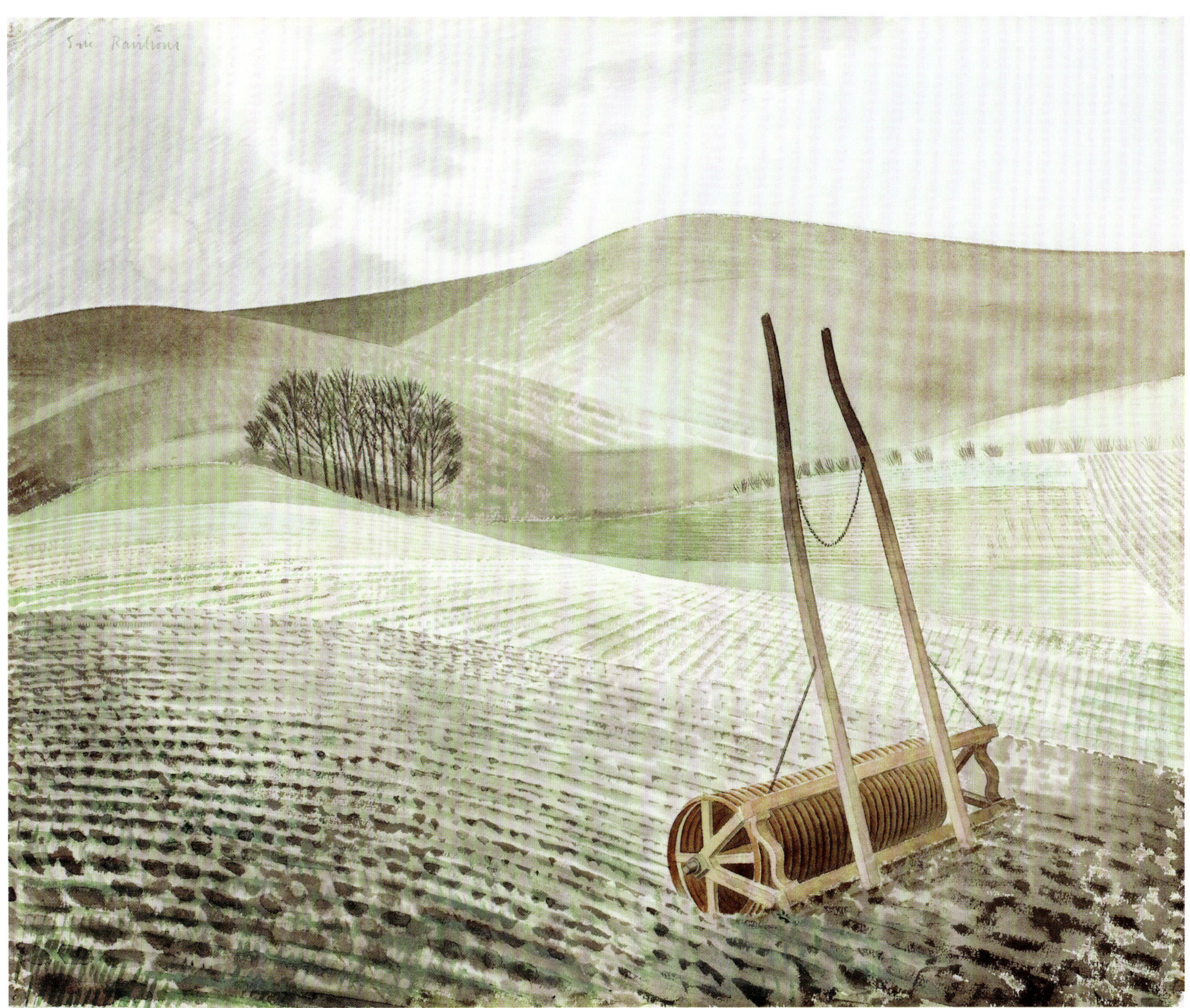

Eric Ravilious

CEMENT WORKS NO. 2

Worlds collide in this unusual portrayal of the South Downs, as rounded hillside is interrupted by industrial buildings. Broken trees hint at John Nash's paintings of the Western Front, but, while sticks and branches litter the foreground, the suggestion of Nature desecrated by Industry is balanced by the bright, clean lines of the works themselves.

When Ravilious first came to Furlongs he had been working on a series of incongruous paintings, showing machinery and abandoned vehicles in the Essex countryside. Now he saw, looking down from Beddingham Hill, the exposed chalk face of the Asham Cement Works. Approaching closer, he was excited by the strangeness of chalk-whitened buildings, dolly engines and a landscape dusted with fine white powder; with Peggy Angus as his guide he went back at night, when work continued by the light of arc lamps and flares.

The pair went to see Mr Wilson, the manager of the works, who was surprised but pleased to meet artists who could see beauty in an industrial operation that others tended to regard as a blot on the landscape. Given free run of the place, they returned together in all weathers to sketch and paint the chalk pits and works, the chimneys, sheds and railway lines.

In this painting, the contrast between pristine buildings and damaged trees suggests some sympathy between the artist and preservationists who had opposed the opening of the cement works in the mid-1920s. Though forgotten now, the battle over the works was a cause célèbre at the time, not least because the new factory engulfed Asham House, where Virginia Woolf lived and worked between 1912 and 1919, and where she wrote *The Voyage Out* before moving across the River Ouse to Rodmell. The house was eventually demolished in 1994, by which time the cement works was closed and the chalk pits put to new use as a landfill site; as of August 2009 the landfill site too has closed and is being capped with chalk, as part of its restoration, bringing the history of this particular place full circle.

No visible trace remains of the Asham Cement Works, a successful business for half a century and the scene of a little-known industrial experiment. In 1928 chemist Geoffrey Martin built a massive kiln within the face of the quarry at Asham, and set about testing a novel method of mixing and firing chalk and clay to make cement. The experiment went nowhere, but the remains of the kiln lie buried underground, waiting to be discovered by archaeologists of the future. They might refer to Ravilious's watercolours: a valuable, and strikingly original, historical record, and a thoughtful depiction of human industry.

Cement Works No. 2, 1934, watercolour, 45.7 x 61.6 cm, Sheffield Galleries and Museums Trust.

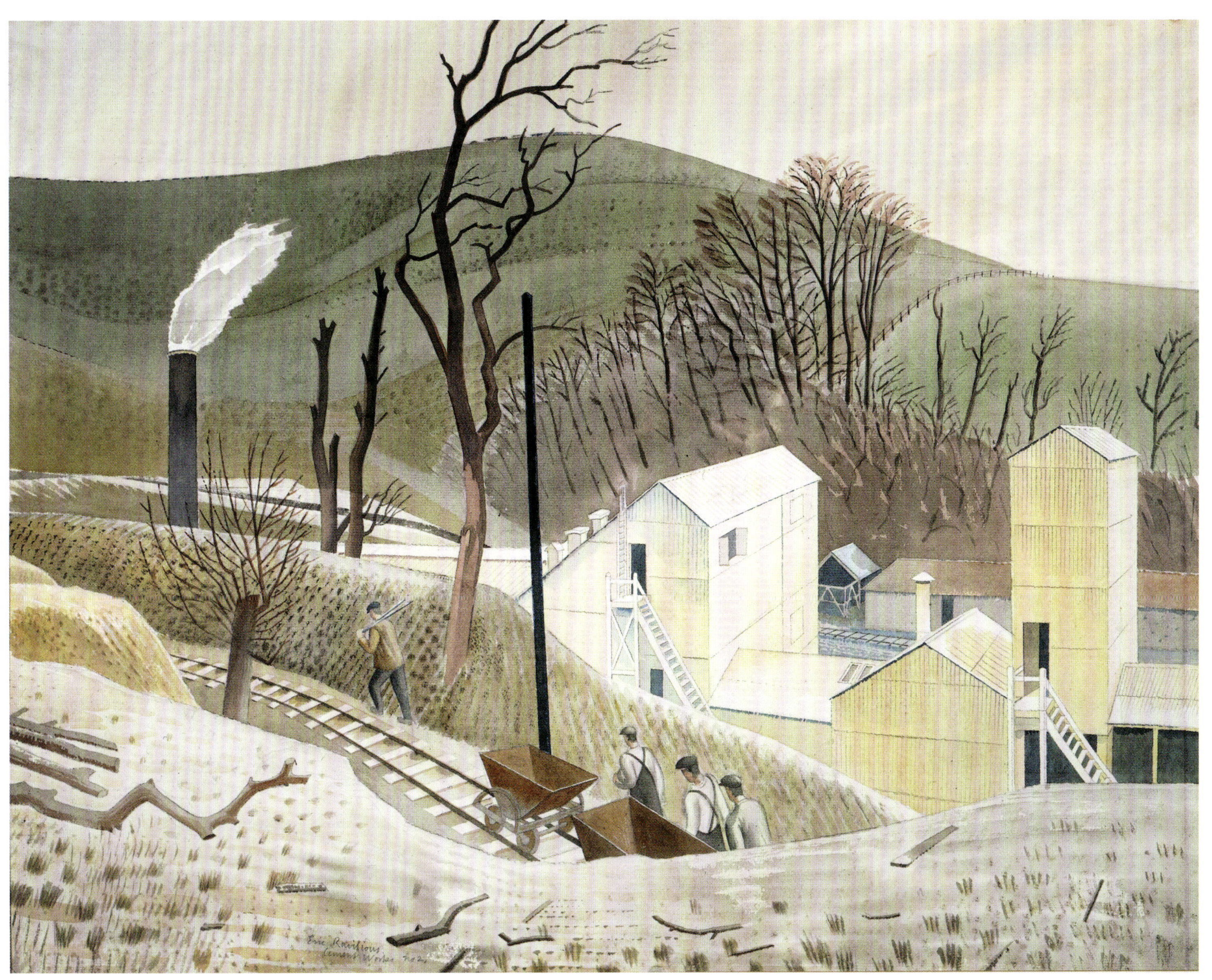

CARAVANS

At the brow of a hill two caravans stand, as if parked by the side of the lane for the night. The track curving up and around, disappearing tantalisingly over the horizon, suggests a journey interrupted, a feeling heightened by the light foliage on the trees; this is spring, a time for travel. But these are not gypsy caravans.

Ravilious and Peggy Angus were walking home after a day painting at the cement works when they spotted two strange-looking vehicles almost concealed among the dust-whitened vegetation of an overgrown lane. Curious, they crawled in closer, finding bunk beds in one van, but no clue as to where the vehicles had come from. So they asked Mr Wilson, who explained that these were fever wagons, used thirty years earlier in the Boer War – or as long ago as the Crimean War, according to Peggy Angus's recollection – and then shipped back to Newhaven. They had been brought up to the cement works when it was first being prospected, he thought, to provide accommodation.

Mr Wilson was happy to be rid of the encumbrance of these old relics, as he put it, and sold them to Ravilious for fifteen shillings each. At the time Eric and Tirzah were house-hunting and had recently discovered Muggery Pope, an empty farmhouse on the far side of Beddingham Hill. Ravilious started a painting of the house but tore it up,

while the house itself turned out to be hopelessly unsuitable, being accessible only by foot and in an advanced state of dereliction. The fever vans, on the other hand, were both serviceable and portable. Ravilious hired a breakdown lorry from Lewes to tow them up the lane to Furlongs, concealing them in the bushes to avoid upsetting the Glynde Estate, and set about restoring them. In reality they stood side by side, hidden from view.

Tirzah painstakingly decorated the caravans, one of which became their bedroom. The other Ravilious converted into a studio, with a skylight and large window looking over Mount Caburn, and a worktable beneath the window. Here the caravans remained, in use until the war and subsequently falling into the derelict condition in which they were photographed by Edwin Smith in the mid-1950s.

Though picturesque to the modern eye the fever van was a familiar sight in British towns and cities of the 1930s, collecting victims of diphtheria and scarlet fever and transporting them to rural isolation hospitals. In 1935 L. S. Lowry made a memorable painting of a fever van parked in a Salford street, surrounded by an anxious crowd. Whereas his painting illustrates the effects of the van's arrival, Ravilious concentrates on the vehicles themselves, conveying in a darkened window a sense of their sombre history, but revelling too in their idiosyncrasy.

Caravans, 1936, watercolour, 45.0 x 56.0 cm, Fry Art Gallery, Saffron Walden.

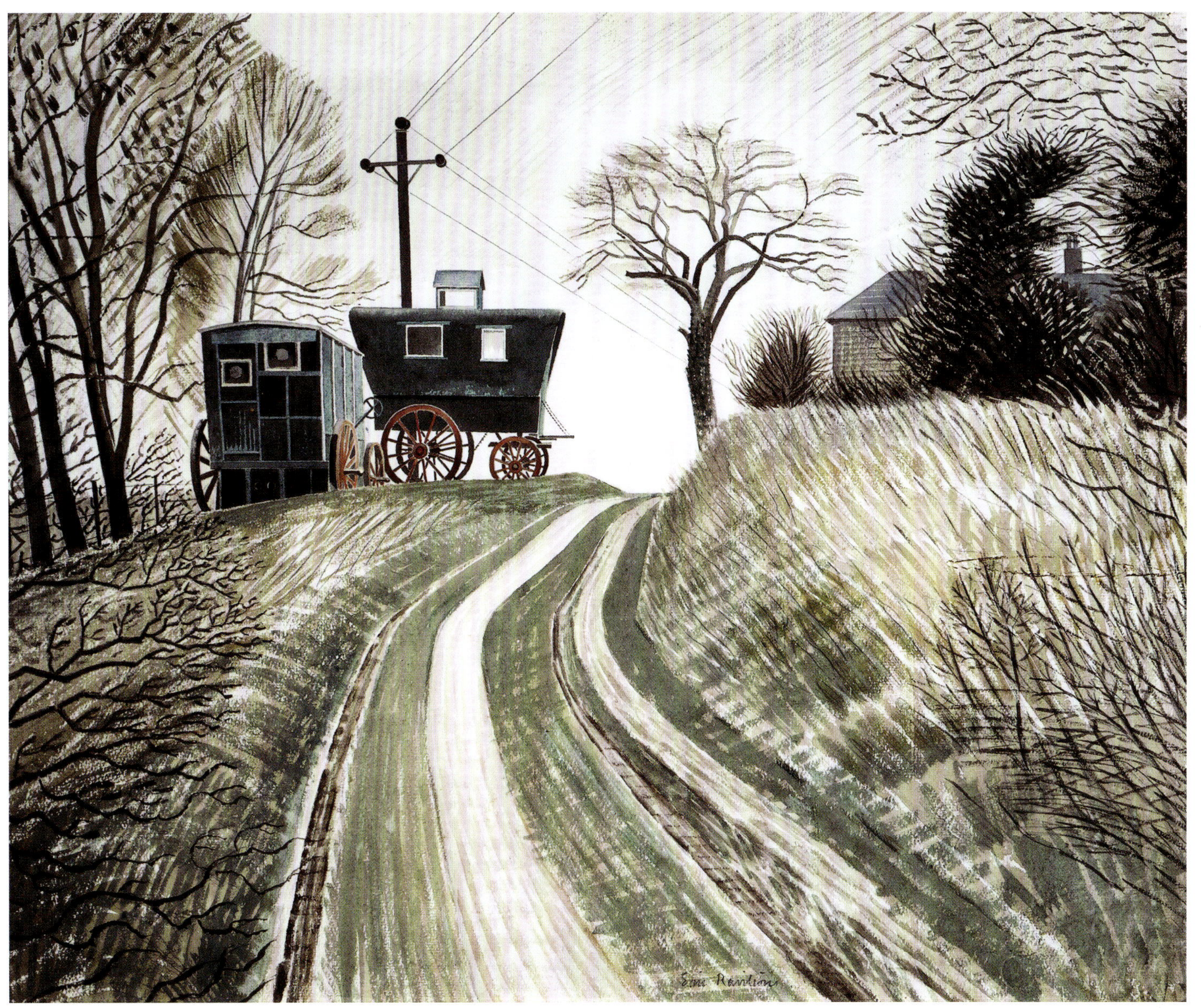

CHALK PATHS

Between the wars the Downs became synonymous with freedom. Then, as now, the chalk hills fascinated people whose homes lay in lowland towns and cities, and they came in increasing numbers by rail, or by car, or by Green Line Coach from London, to experience the wide skies and breezes. As early as 1903 Edward Thomas had written enticingly of the Sussex Downs in *The South Country*, describing his escape from London by train to 'this pure kingdom of grass and sky'. To Thomas, the chalk paths were filled with mystery and promise.

'The long white roads are a temptation,' he wrote. 'What quests they propose! They take us away to the thin air of the future or to the underworld of the past.'

Eric Ravilious once remarked that he never knew the date at Furlongs, and he was not alone in relishing the freedom of life there. Here he conveys the airy, open quality of the landscape, and the lure of the white road, although this vision of freedom seems circumscribed by the taut black barbed-wire fence that separates us from the path. We may be unwise to look for a meaning in this fence, but its presence adds to the painting a certain quality of unease.

Subjects like this seemed plentiful in the country around Furlongs, a landscape that fascinated and inspired Ravilious like no other. Experiencing it, he told Peggy Angus, changed his whole outlook and his way of painting, 'I think because the colour of the landscape was so lovely and the design so beautifully obvious'.

He got up early, often at dawn, and set off carrying his drawing board in a large brown canvas satchel made for him by Tirzah. A tall figure, with a brown round-brimmed hat pulled firmly down on his head, he would stride off across the Downs, stopping to work either standing, at a light sketching easel, or else seated with the board across his knees. Returning to Furlongs at midday, he ate mutton or eggs for lunch and rested for a while before going back to work more on the painting he had begun earlier; he had an uncanny ability to retain his intense first impression of a subject, however the light or weather might change.

Often, pressure of time or vagaries in the weather meant Ravilious had to finish drawings in his caravan-studio — or even back in Essex — from notes pencilled onto the paper. But this seemed if anything to enhance his vision, in which a topographer's eye was combined with a keen sense of the visual possibilities in a landscape. The creative power of memory allowed him to get beyond geographical details and, as he does here, capture the spirit of a place.

Chalk Paths, 1935, watercolour, 47.0 x 56.5 cm, private collection.

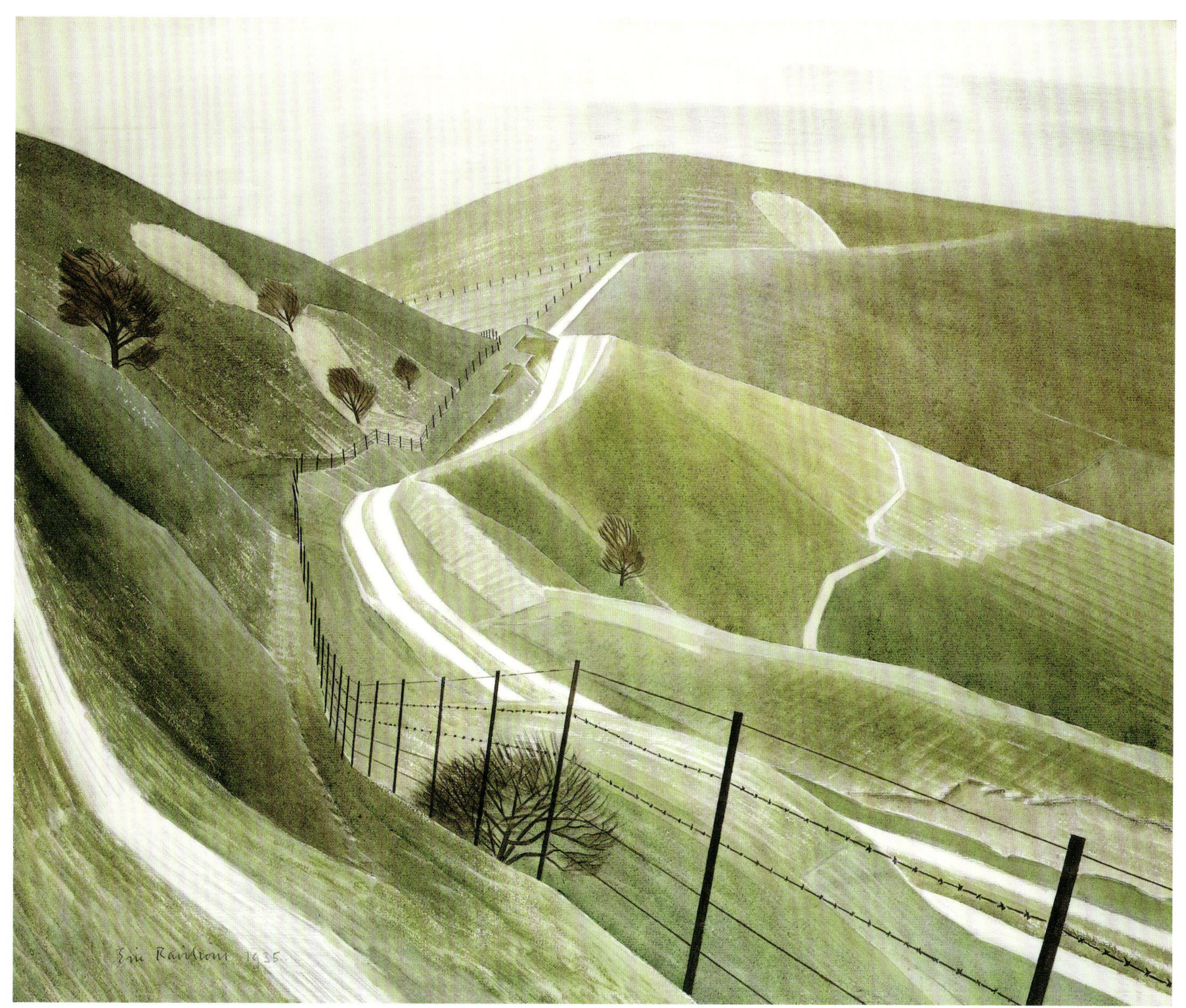

THE GREENHOUSE

As yellow tomatoes ripen on the vine above, twin lines of cyclamen in orange pots draw us through one open doorway then another, until we are faced by the final, closed door, so pale and faint it seems to float just above the centre of the picture. In startling contrast to the wide open spaces of paintings such as 'The Waterwheel' or 'Downs in Winter', this greenhouse pulls us into an intense interior world. Not that this is an oppressive space. Light and airy, apparently roofed with nothing more substantial than tomato plants, the greenhouse offers a pleasant dream of infinite regression.

While exploring the village of Firle, Ravilious stumbled upon this horticultural treasure, one of eight greenhouses concealed within a walled garden built to supply Firle Place with fresh produce. Along the walls grew espaliered fruit trees, including the celebrated greengages first introduced to Britain in the 18th century by Sir William Gage, while the hothouses included a mushroom house and a rare Victorian strawberry house in which plants grew in the warm air close to the roof and were lowered by pulley for picking.

This fabulous kitchen garden was watched over by the bearded head gardener, Mr Humphreys, who had, as a young man, travelled up the Amazon on a journey of botanical discovery. Ravilious befriended him and went on to paint several of the greenhouses, creating a monument to these elegant structures.

You can buy tomatoes from the same greenhouse today, from a stall across from the Firle Stores, though the rest have all but disappeared. In 1944 a Spitfire brought down a doodlebug nearby and the resulting explosion shattered every pane of glass in the village; the walled garden never fully recovered. The great storm of October 1987 caused further destruction, plucking whole polytunnels from the ground and spiriting them away.

But this one greenhouse survives, lovingly maintained and tended by Firle native Jim Piper. He remembers what the garden was like when he was a boy, when his mother was nurse to the Gage family, but though in his seventies, he is too young to remember Mr Humphreys. He does, however, tell a story of that botanist's later years. Old-fashioned in dress and outlook, Mr Humphreys was the object of good-natured taunts from village lads, delivered from the safety of the churchyard beyond the garden wall.

'None of you buggers knows anything about hard work,' he liked to retort. 'But when I snuff it you'll have to work bloody hard because I'm going under that yew tree.'

Sure enough his grave can be found only yards from the garden, in the tough tangle of roots beneath the churchyard yew.

The Greenhouse: Cyclamen and Tomatoes, 1935, watercolour, 47.0 x 59.7 cm, Tate, London.

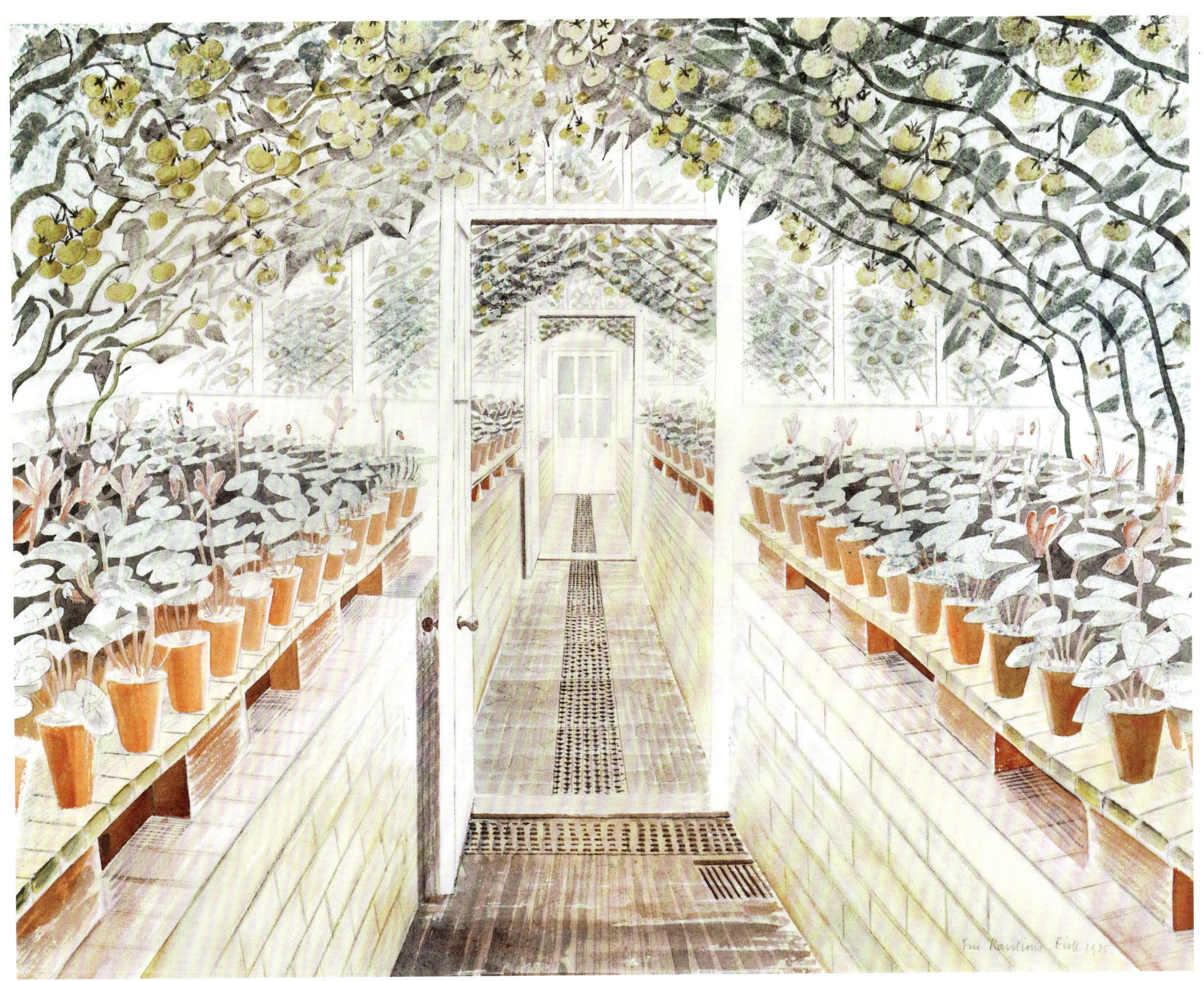

Eric Ravilious Frith 1935

In 'Firle Beacon' the landscape beyond the fence is loosely sketched, but here it is described close up, in detail, with the precision and fascination for place that Gilbert White showed in his writing. This is the reverse of the view in 'Furlongs', with the cottage and its neighbouring haystack seen from the lower slopes of Beddingham Hill, alongside the barns and buildings of a substantial farm.

With a peak a hundred and fifty metres above sea level, Mount Caburn hardly seems worthy of its lofty name, and in the local vicinity it is known simply as the Caburn, from the Celtic 'caer bryn', or 'stronghold hill'. But it is one of those hills that gains authority from being solitary, divided from the South Downs proper by Glynde Reach, a tributary of the Ouse. A well-known Sussex landmark, Caburn bears on its crown the remains of a Bronze Age hill fort and the scars of numerous archaeological excavations. On 6 May 1935 a bonfire was lit on the summit to celebrate the Silver Jubilee of George V, a spectacle Ravilious was sorry to miss, having returned to Essex the previous week to engrave a menu design for the Double Crown Club.

Like cottage and farm, the field pictured belongs to the Glynde Estate and the men were its tenants and labourers: one is almost certainly Mr Barnes, the ploughman Ravilious observed out with the roller in a winter storm. Here the roller is shown in action, pulled by a team of horses. Another team pulls a harrow, while the solitary and almost imperceptible figure in the distance is sowing seed. This may seem a nostalgic picture, but in 1935 half a million Shire horses worked on English farms; only after World War II did the tractor take over.

Mr and Mrs Barnes lived next door to Furlongs and, like the postman who handed letters in through the open window, and Mrs Soames the laundress, they were an integral part of life there. Although Ravilious was grateful to these neighbours for sustenance on more than one occasion, relations were not always good, and in April 1935, while he was working on this painting, there was a frightful row. Some sheets, a saw and other items had gone missing from the cottage and Ravilious delivered a note to Mr Barnes on the subject. Mrs Barnes stormed in, protesting her innocence — yet somehow managing to produce the missing saw — and then had a fit. Ravilious carried her to the sofa, writing afterwards, 'That business was a pity… and I'd have liked her more if she had hurled them all in at us instead of collapsing on the sofa.'

With the help of fellow guest Jim Richards, he bought and fitted a new lock. The key was hidden in the outhouse.

Mount Caburn, 1935, watercolour, 47.0 x 58.2 cm, private collection.

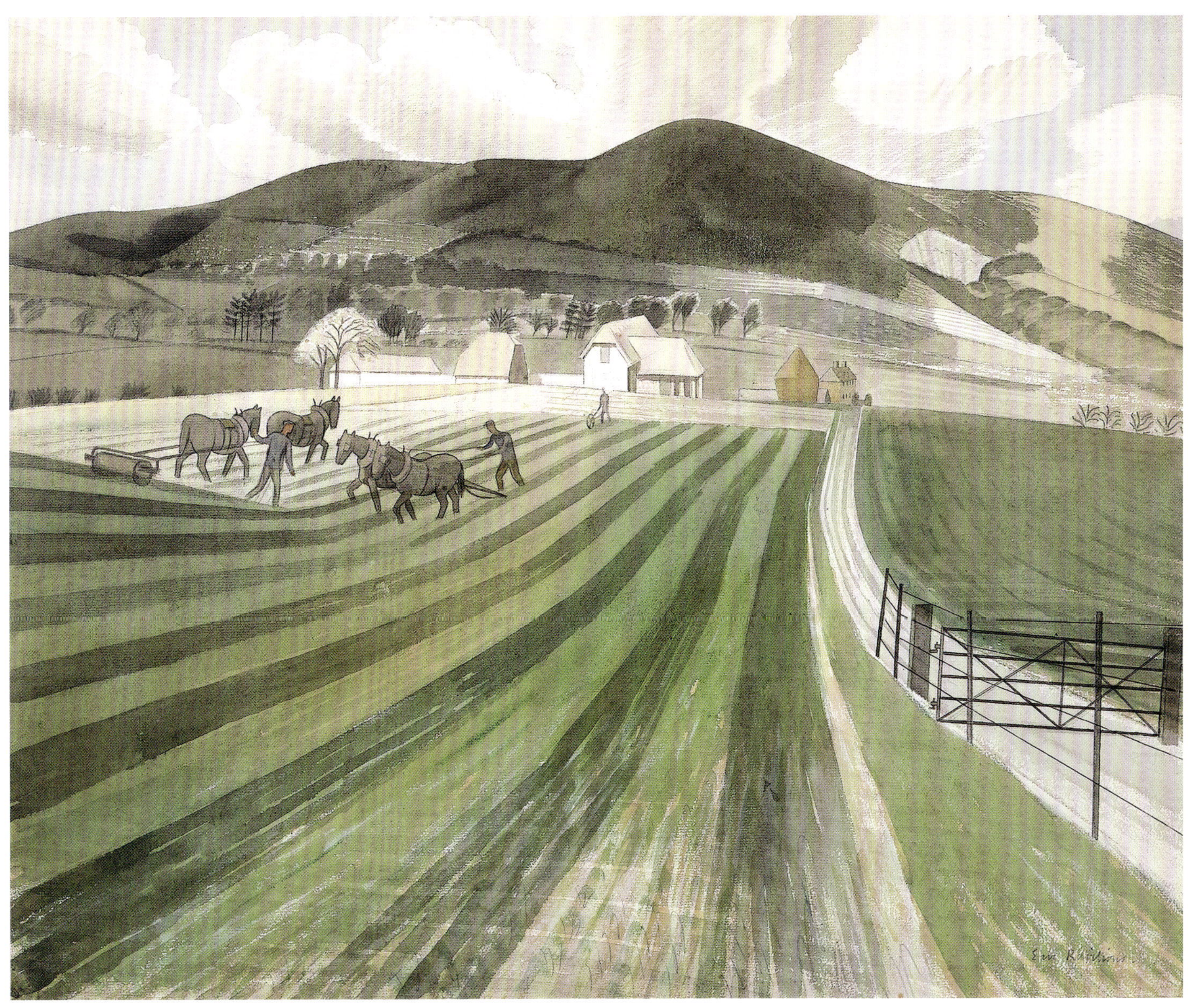

WILTSHIRE LANDSCAPE

The open road held 1930s Britain in thrall. Though Ravilious never learned to drive, his contemporaries were taking to the road in ever-increasing numbers, encouraged by advertisements and guidebooks that portrayed an idealised vision of the countryside. The *Shell Guides*, sponsored by the oil company and edited by John Betjeman, were aimed specifically at the new breed of car-driving metropolitan tourist, with highlights including Betjeman's *Devon* (1935), Paul Nash's *Dorset* (1936) and John Piper's *Oxon* (1938). The worse London's traffic jams became, the greater the appeal of open country.

Ravilious himself produced a number of wood engravings to advertise London Transport and its offshoot Green Line Buses, and in 1936 made engravings for the first two books of *Country Walks*, which described and mapped forty walks accessible by bus or coach from central London. Not that the artist had an aversion to cars. He once told Helen Binyon he wished they could drive fifty miles as fast as possible then go dancing afterwards. And in March 1937, shortly before painting 'Wiltshire Landscape', he noted that 'Tirzah is buying a year-old Morris for £70 tomorrow from the local garage, and it seems to my eye to look as good as new. May it start up in cold weather.'

While contemporary guidebooks and advertising focused on sights to be seen along the road, this painting shows the road itself, from an odd, slightly raised perspective. The spring countryside is peripheral, and instead one's attention focuses on the junction ahead and the red van approaching from the left. In fact Ravilious did not see this vehicle on the road but spotted it in a Post Office magazine when he got home and added it to the composition.

Imagine the picture without it and the mood is rather different, the road stretching ahead perhaps less a route to freedom than a journey to be endured; hemmed in by endless green verges, only the turning to the left offers respite.

A similar melancholy pervades 'The Causeway, Wiltshire Downs', the other painting from this short trip. As a non-driver Ravilious relied on public transport or the good will of friends, and in April 1937 Helen Binyon was his driver and companion. They stayed near Andover and drove out across Salisbury Plain, but it was not the kind of great adventure they had enjoyed in the past. Binyon was silent and distant, Ravilious said afterwards, which made him 'uppish and out of hand'; a month later he was to end their long-running affair, though they remained close friends.

But this is still an image of the open road – the kind of byway that city dwellers dreamt (and dream) of. The clouds may be grey and stormy but the road ahead gleams silver.

Wiltshire Landscape, 1937, watercolour, 41.9 x 54.6 cm, private collection.

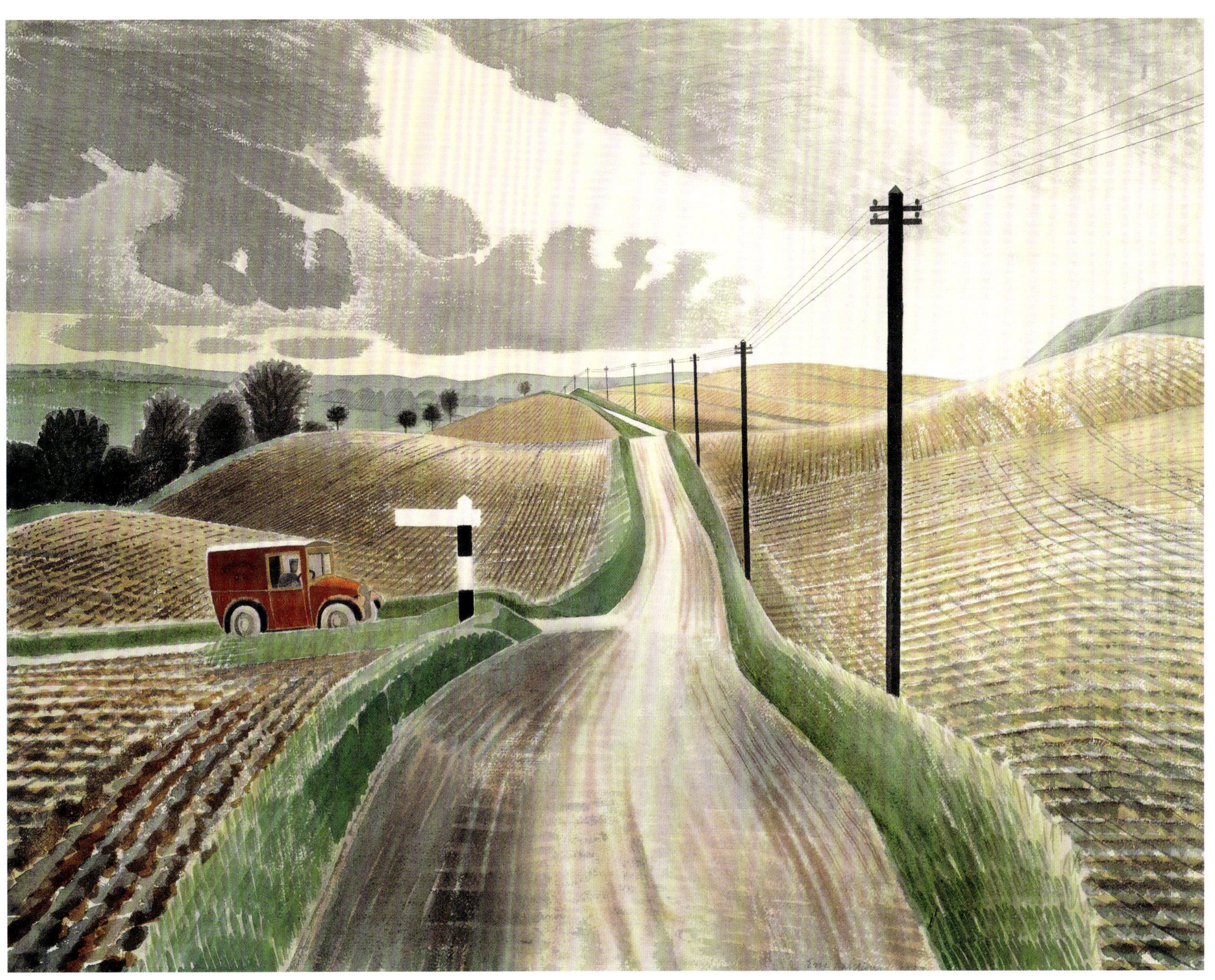

BEACHY HEAD

A precursor to the extended series of coastal views Ravilious undertook as a war artist, 'Beachy Head' offers a unique vision of a famous landmark. Few images symbolise England more succinctly than the chalk cliffs of the Channel coast – the name Albion may derive from their whiteness – and in this painting the counterbalanced areas of colour and sharply defined angles give the ancient landscape a modern voice. Light bursts in all directions from the lighthouse and, although this is a night scene, the land and sky are stippled with points of light, while the cliffs and sea are radiant.

The famous headland takes its name from the French, 'Beauchef' or 'beautiful headland', but to sailors it was always a hazard. The first lighthouse, Belle Tout, was built on the adjacent cliffs in the early 1830s, but with sea mists frequently obscuring its light a new lighthouse was constructed at the base of Beachy Head; materials and workers were lowered by cable car from the clifftops. It began operating in 1902, sending out two flashes of light every twenty seconds, while Belle Tout was decommissioned and converted into a house.

In the spring of 1939 Ravilious stayed with his parents in Eastbourne and went out, with Tirzah the uncomplaining chauffeur, to paint the surrounding country. On 10 May his Exhibition of Recent Watercolours was to open at Arthur Tooth and Sons' gallery in New Bond Street, so he approached the work with urgency and, knowing the area well, sought out unusual viewpoints for his paintings. One day he spent 'sitting in a magnificent Chinese chair' in the lantern of the disused Belle Tout lighthouse, 'drawing the immense expanse below with a gale blowing outside', another perched 'on a projecting bit of cliff about four yards square, but flat and comfortable'. Richard Jefferies once waxed lyrical about the breezes of Beachy Head, but Ravilious found his music in the light. 'An immense bar of light on the sea is splendid,' he enthused, 'and must be done.'

With paintings like this on display the show at Tooth's was a resounding success. In an adjoining room was an exhibition of oil paintings by Sir Timothy Eden, brother of Conservative MP Anthony Eden, and Ravilious was very amused when the doorman told him, 'You can see which are your people – they look more intelligent.' Critics in *The Observer* and *The Sunday Times* were impressed, leaving Ravilious feeling 'set up and a bit above myself, like Balbus, whose head was crowned with a garland. This is a kind of reward,' he added in a letter to Helen Binyon shortly after the show's opening, 'for the lumbago and the March winds on Beachy Head.'

Beachy Head, 1939, watercolour, 57.1 x 72.7 cm, private collection.

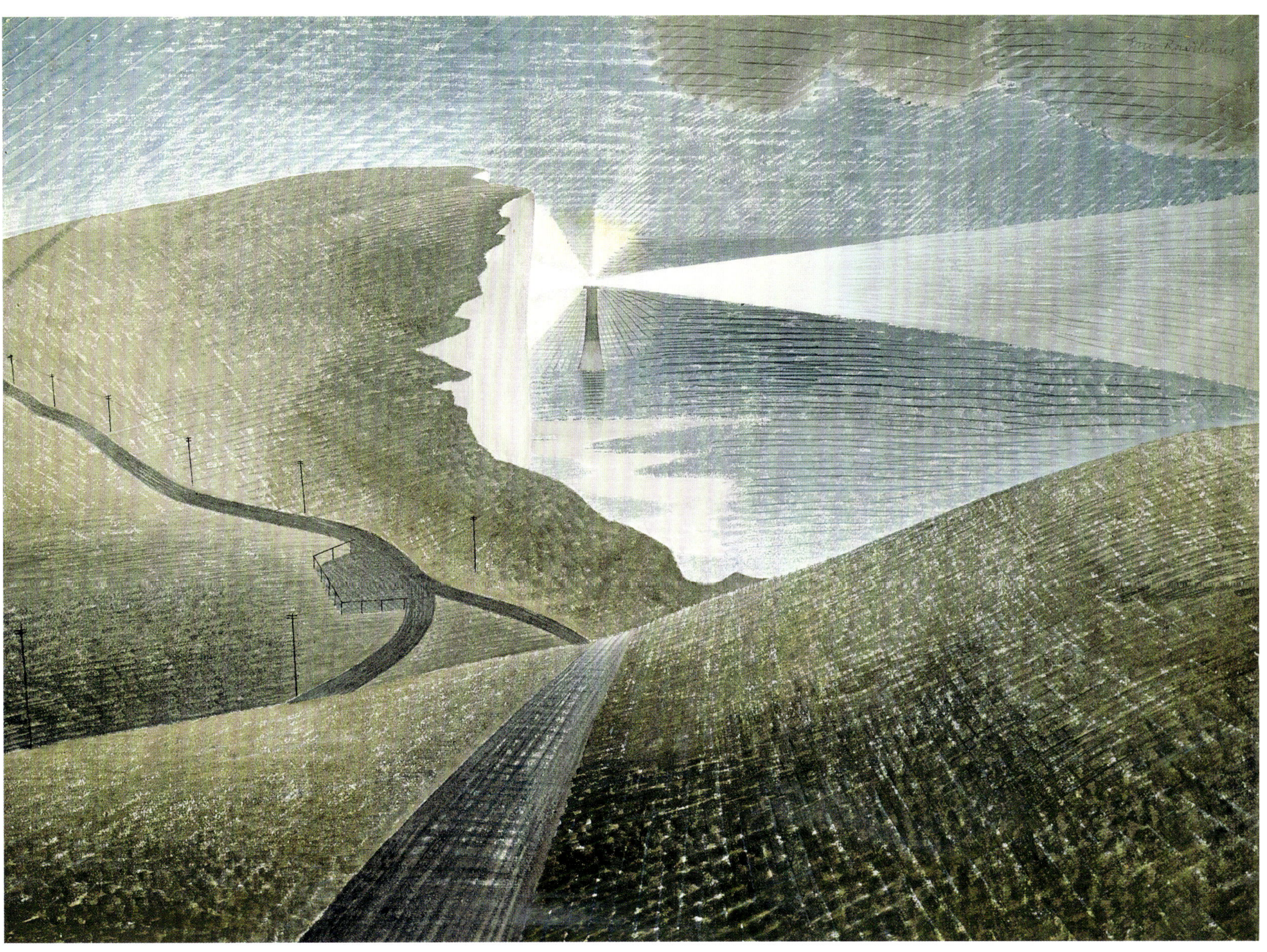

CUCKMERE HAVEN

The Sussex Downs are defined as much by the rivers that divide the hills as they are by the hills themselves. The Arun, Adur, Ouse and Cuckmere wind through broad, fertile valleys, giving the region its distinctive Saxon villages and offering the Downland walker a series of tantalising views. Here Ravilious offers one such, looking south over the famous meanders of the Cuckmere valley. He made the drawing in March, a few months before World War II broke out, and one can see evidence of winter flooding in the numerous small, twisting streams covering the valley floor.

At first sight this seems like a rare instance of Ravilious choosing a natural wonder as his subject, but this landscape is man-made. Across the middle of the drawing, just beyond the second meander, a dark line marks the bank of an artificial cut, excavated in 1846 for reasons that are not completely clear, but are probably related to navigation. Earlier, shipping followed the curves of the river upstream and down, but silting made this increasingly difficult, and today the river flows along the artificial channel, leaving the meanders cut off, like a man-made ox-bow lake. So distinctive are these languid loops that they seem as permanent as the Seven Sisters – the chalk cliffs to the east – but the estuary and the meanders are kept as they are by

flood defences that have to be constantly maintained. In fact the cliffs too keep changing, as they are eroded at the rate of thirty to forty centimetres a year.

When war was declared this valley became a scene of frantic activity, as tank traps, pill boxes and other invasion defences were hastily constructed. Then, as the rest of the country was plunged into the darkness of the blackout, the valley was filled with lights, in the hope that German pilots would mistake it for Newhaven.

It is perhaps fitting that this watercolour shows the artist at his coolest and most modern. As a skilled lithographer and designer of ceramics Ravilious had no fear of artifice, and the cross-hatching in the foreground and across the luminous grey belly of the clouds reflects the man-made quality of the place. Yet the myriad streams covering the valley floor are shown in their natural confusion, and the drawing as a whole is suffused with emotion. Following the languid curves of the river towards the distant sea one might remember Ravilious's fondness for Tom Sawyer and Huckleberry Finn, characters for whom the river spelt freedom and adventure. As in 'Chalk Paths', there is a powerful sense here both of yearning and of wonder; the river is a road and the road leads into the distant blue of the unknown.

Cuckmere Haven, 1939, watercolour, 37.0 x 50.5 cm, private collection, on loan to the Towner Art Gallery, Eastbourne.

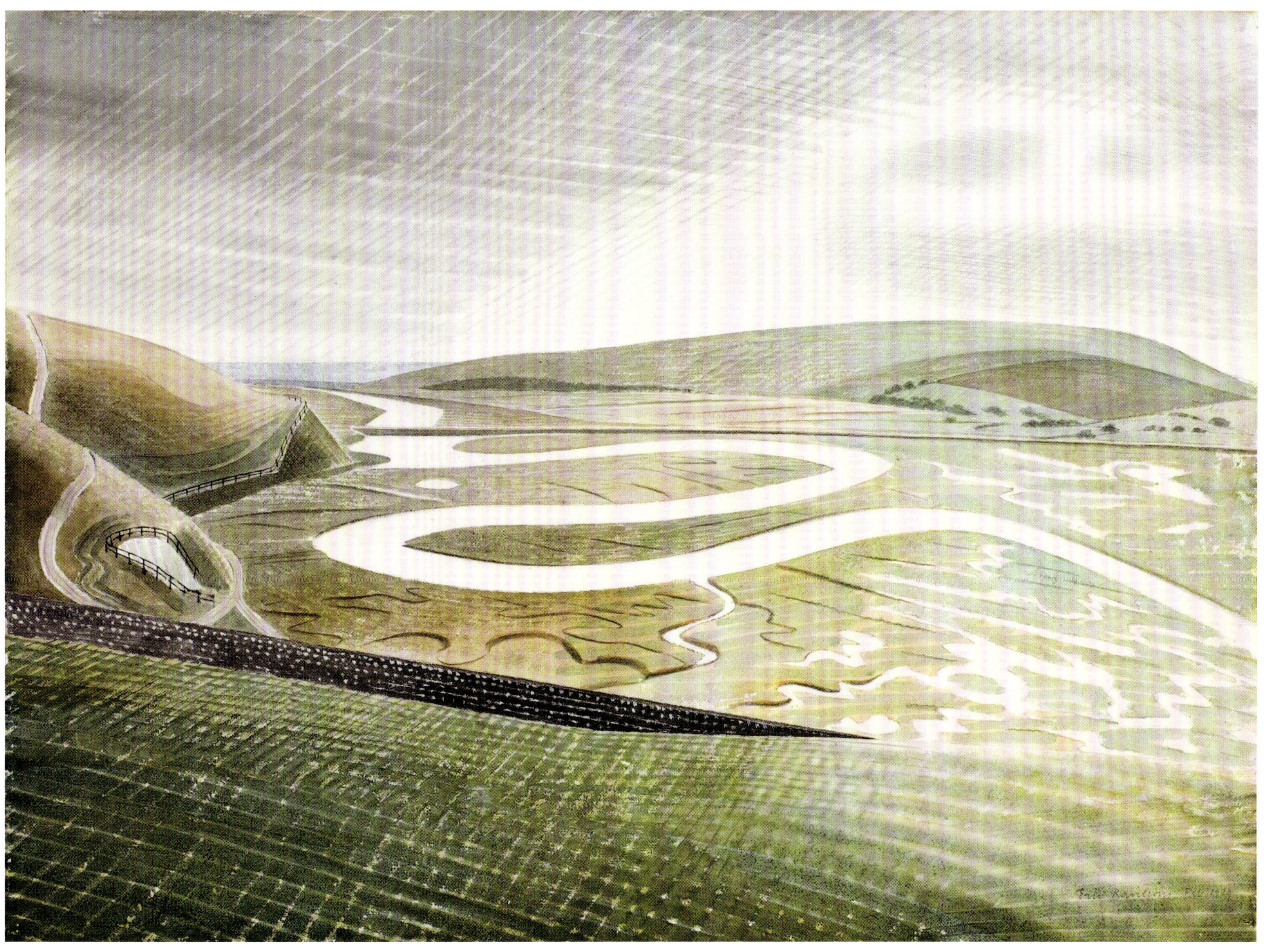

TEA AT FURLONGS

A table laid for two stands in the corner of the flint-walled garden at Furlongs. To another artist this might have been a backdrop, but here the teapot and attendant mugs, bread and butter and bone-handled knives are themselves the focus of a painting that radiates light and pleasure. Only the dark grey umbrella, raised incongruously against the sun, reminds us that this scene is set in August 1939, on the eve of war.

Ravilious was, according to Tirzah, inordinately fond of tea, and returned to the subject on several occasions during his career. His wood engraving of a garden tea table advertised London Transport's Green Line Coach service to Whipsnade in 1936, and a year later he designed a service for Wedgwood entitled 'Afternoon Tea', with beautifully decorative illustrations made specifically for teapot and preserve jar; for the teapot itself he drew a miniature table with a tiny tea service on the top.

Here, though, the tea things are plain, with mismatched teapot and farmhouse milk jug. The chairs do not match either, and with the umbrella-sunshade the overall effect is one of artistic rusticity, eccentric but not overdone. Objects are portrayed in loving detail, particularly the chair on the left, with that distinctive star pattern on the cane seat. In 1936 Ravilious had designed a set of four chairs for Dunbar Hay, a London shop specialising in objects of applied art, using unstained mahogany inlaid with boxwood. He had found these bentwood chairs, meanwhile, in a Lewes junk shop.

One might suppose, from his focus on objects rather than the people who used them, that Ravilious was unsociable. Some contemporaries did find him distracted, as if his mind were elsewhere, but he was more commonly remembered as fun-loving and gregarious, particularly by women. The artist loved the company of women and was inspired and emboldened by the women he loved, from his wife Tirzah to Diana Tuely and Helen Binyon, his companion on many visits to Furlongs and a sensitive, witty biographer. Here his partner in tea may be Peggy Angus, with whom he was staying in August 1939.

Angus was heavily pregnant and when she went into labour one night Ravilious was dispatched by bike to the phone box in Glynde. He called a doctor who had been to the house before, but the doctor remembered the lack of electricity or running water and refused to come out. Instead Ravilious roused Mr Lusted, landlord of the Trevor Arms, by throwing stones at his window, and persuaded him to drive the pair of them to a nursing home in Lewes.

'How we laughed on that journey,' Peggy Angus remembered later. 'An adventure to tell round the fire.'

Tea at Furlongs, 1939, watercolour, 45.8 x 56.0 cm, Fry Art Gallery, Saffron Walden.

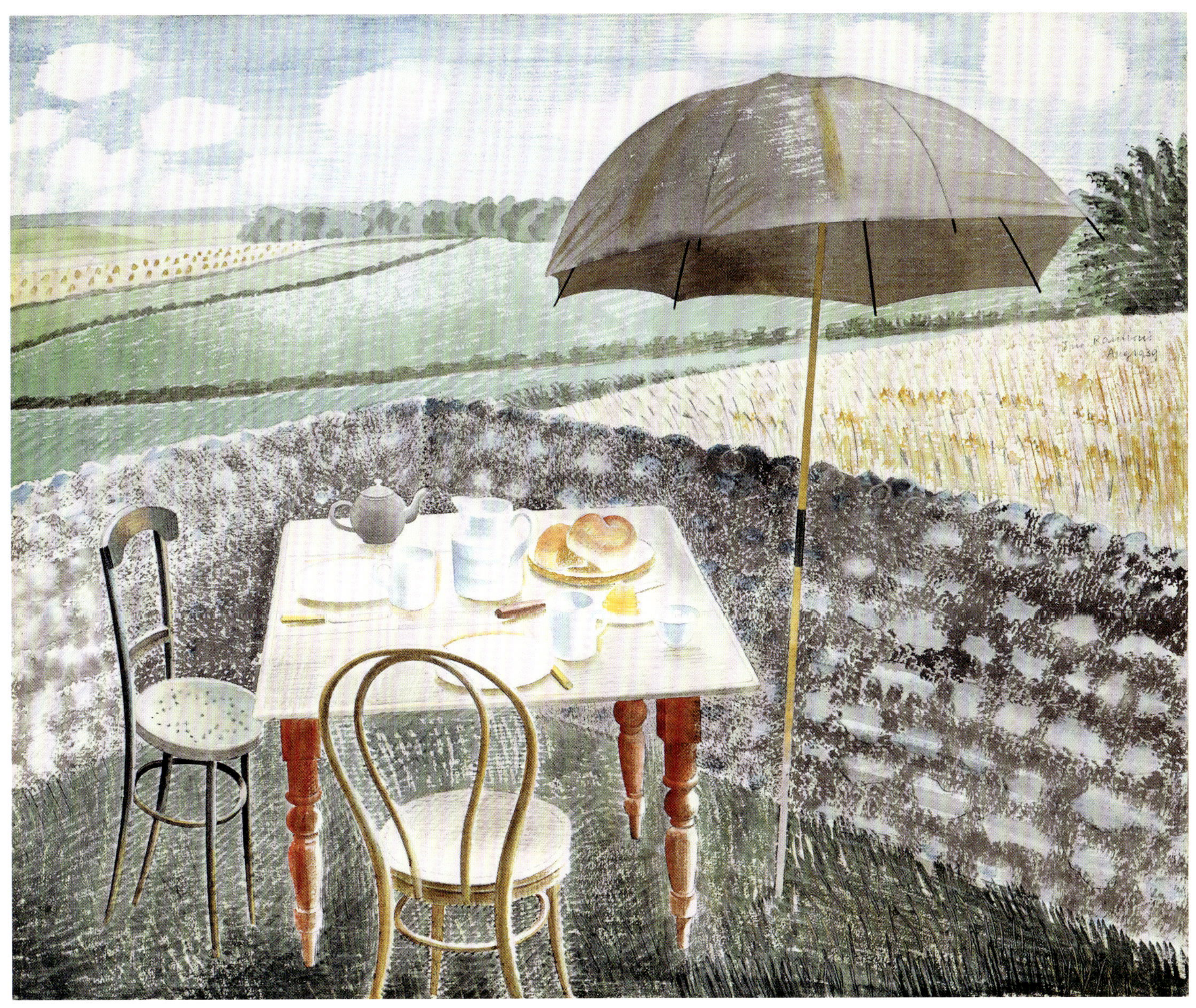

England is traditionally a country of hedgerows and dry stone walls, in which the barbed-wire fence is a modern interloper. Patented in the United States in 1868, barbed wire was widely used by Downland farmers as they reclaimed land for agriculture, and Ravilious saw and exploited its aesthetic qualities. Here the antique chalk figure is framed by fence posts and wire, which draw us into the painting and around a distant curve to the feet of the giant.

Wilmington was one of the villages Ravilious visited with students from Eastbourne Art School, and he portrayed the giant, or Long Man, in different media: in two of the wood engravings he made for the *Lanston Monotype Almanack* of 1929, and also in the Morley College murals that were unveiled by Prime Minister Stanley Baldwin the following year. In August 1939, while staying with Peggy Angus at Furlongs, he made this watercolour, which was bought a year later by the V&A. Ravilious's decision to paint this subject at this time was perceptive, since public interest in archaeology, stimulated by the discovery of Tutankhamun's tomb in 1922, reached fever pitch in the summer of 1939 when the remains of a Saxon burial ship were uncovered at Sutton Hoo in Suffolk. Anxious about the future, people became more fascinated than ever by the mysteries of the past.

And the Wilmington Giant is an enigma. First recorded in 1710, and perhaps carved into the turf of Windover Hill not long before, the figure stands 226 feet tall, making it one of the world's largest representations of the human figure. But is this Baldr, the Norse sun god, pushing aside the gates of darkness? Or a pilgrim, advertising the Priory below? Ravilious had his own, rather exotic interpretation, comparing the figure to a depiction of Virgo by Bartolo di Fredi, the 14th-century Italian painter, and suggesting that the giant was really a giantess. He might have enjoyed a recent TV stunt, in which eighty women, dressed in white, lay down in formation on the hillside to turn the Long Man into the Long Woman.

Curiously, in 1941 Ravilious was travelling by train to London when he met 'a long elderly high collared man of about fifty' who said he owned the Wilmington Giant, and described turfing it over at the Air Ministry's request. It was the kind of encounter on trains that Ravilious liked, but who was the old gentleman? Along with Wilmington Priory, the giant had been donated to the Sussex Archaeological Trust more than fifteen years earlier by the 9th Duke of Devonshire, who died in 1938. So was this stranger on the train the 10th Duke, Edward William Spencer Cavendish, or an archaeologist with delusions of grandeur?

The Wilmington Giant, 1939, watercolour, 44.7 x 53.7 cm, Victoria and Albert Museum, London.

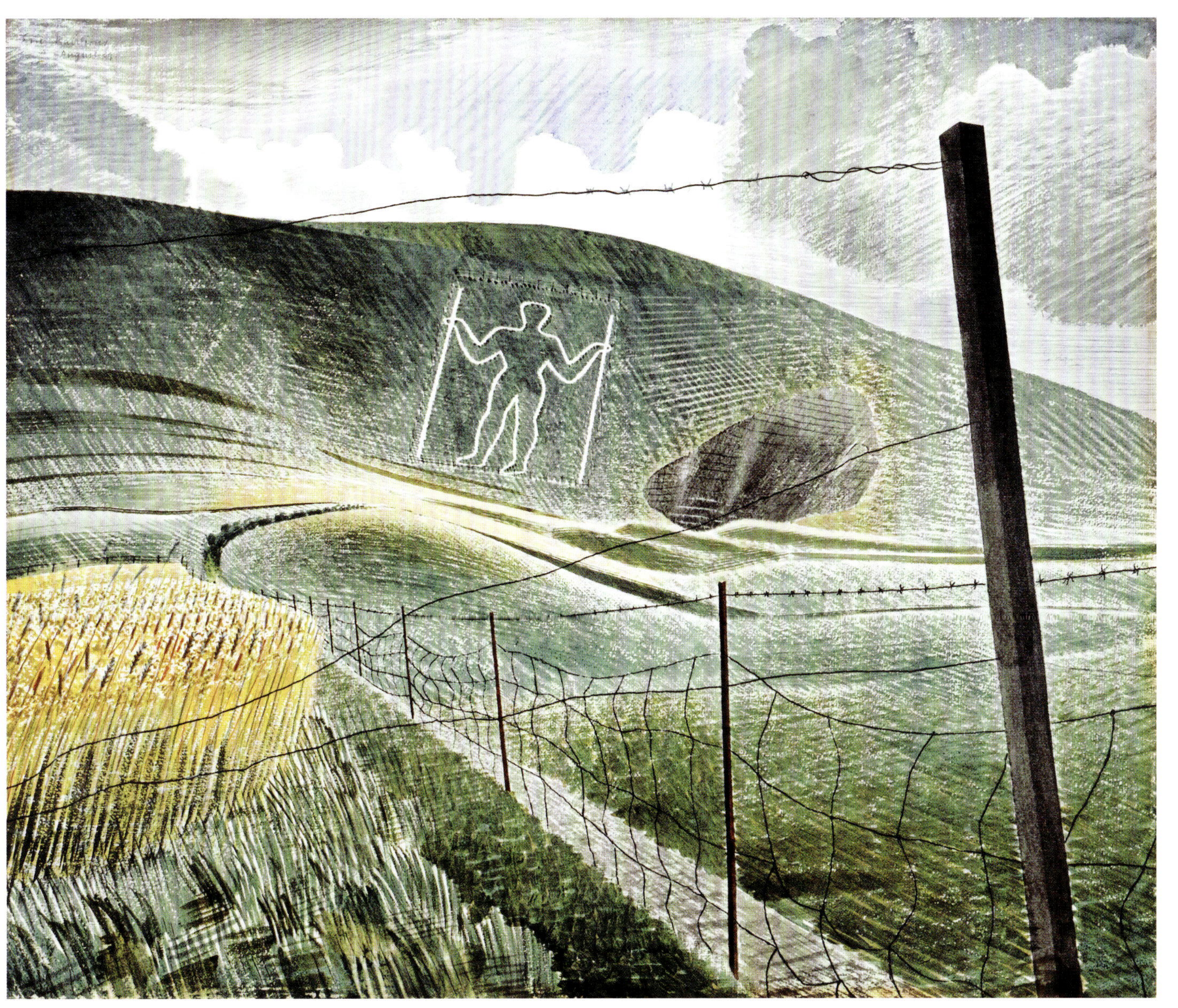

THE WESTBURY HORSE

Wiltshire abounds in white horses, with eight currently visible. In 1778 this monumental figure was carved into the earth ramparts of Bratton Camp, an Iron Age fort on Westbury Hill, probably over an older horse that had legendary associations with King Alfred. Ravilious chose a well-known vantage point on the same hill for this painting, looking down across the valley of the River Avon; a train steams across the pale grid of fields below, setting up an intriguing contrast of ancient and modern. With its boxy wagons, this train resembles illustrations of toy trains by Tirzah Ravilious, and it may be relevant that Eric, who shared her interest in toys and models, included W. J. Bassett-Lowke's famous Holborn model shop in *High Street*, his book of shops.

Perhaps he painted the train in his studio, with a toy for his model, but he began the watercolour on site, during an intensive painting tour. After making a successful start with the Wilmington Giant he had decided to paint more figures in September 1939, but war intervened. Joining the Observer Corps, Ravilious stayed in Essex until early December, when he abruptly swapped shifts with a fellow Observer and rushed off. He had been promised a job drawing chalk figures for a book, he told Diana Tuely, and in a tremendous burst of energy drew the white horses of Uffington and Westbury, the Cerne Abbas Giant and George III on horseback outside Weymouth.

On his return, he was invited to be a war artist — 'a sort of Christmas present from the Admiralty', as he described it. Like John Nash he was awarded the honorary rank of Captain in the Royal Marines, and sent to paint suitable subjects. The book of horses and giants was not forgotten, however, and in January 1941 he sent a dummy to Noel Carrington, who was then editing the Picture Puffin series of children's books for Penguin. Carrington responded enthusiastically, suggesting that the book might include drawings not only of chalk figures, earthworks and castles, but also of implements excavated from prehistoric sites. 'Downland Man' or 'Whitehorse Hill' might be the title, with accompanying text by H. J. Massingham; artist and author had collaborated not long before, when Ravilious illustrated Massingham's new edition of *The Natural History of Selborne* by Gilbert White.

With Tirzah about to have a third child, Anne, Ravilious decided not to proceed, but he continued to work on the book and, according to Carrington, took the dummy with him on his posting to Iceland in August 1942, intending to finish it. Presumed lost, the artefact reappeared in 2012 when artist Roland Collins revealed that Carrington had given it to him during a post-war office move. It now resides, fittingly, at the Wiltshire Museum.

The Westbury Horse, 1939, watercolour, 44.4 x 54.6 cm, private collection, on loan to the Towner Art Gallery, Eastbourne.

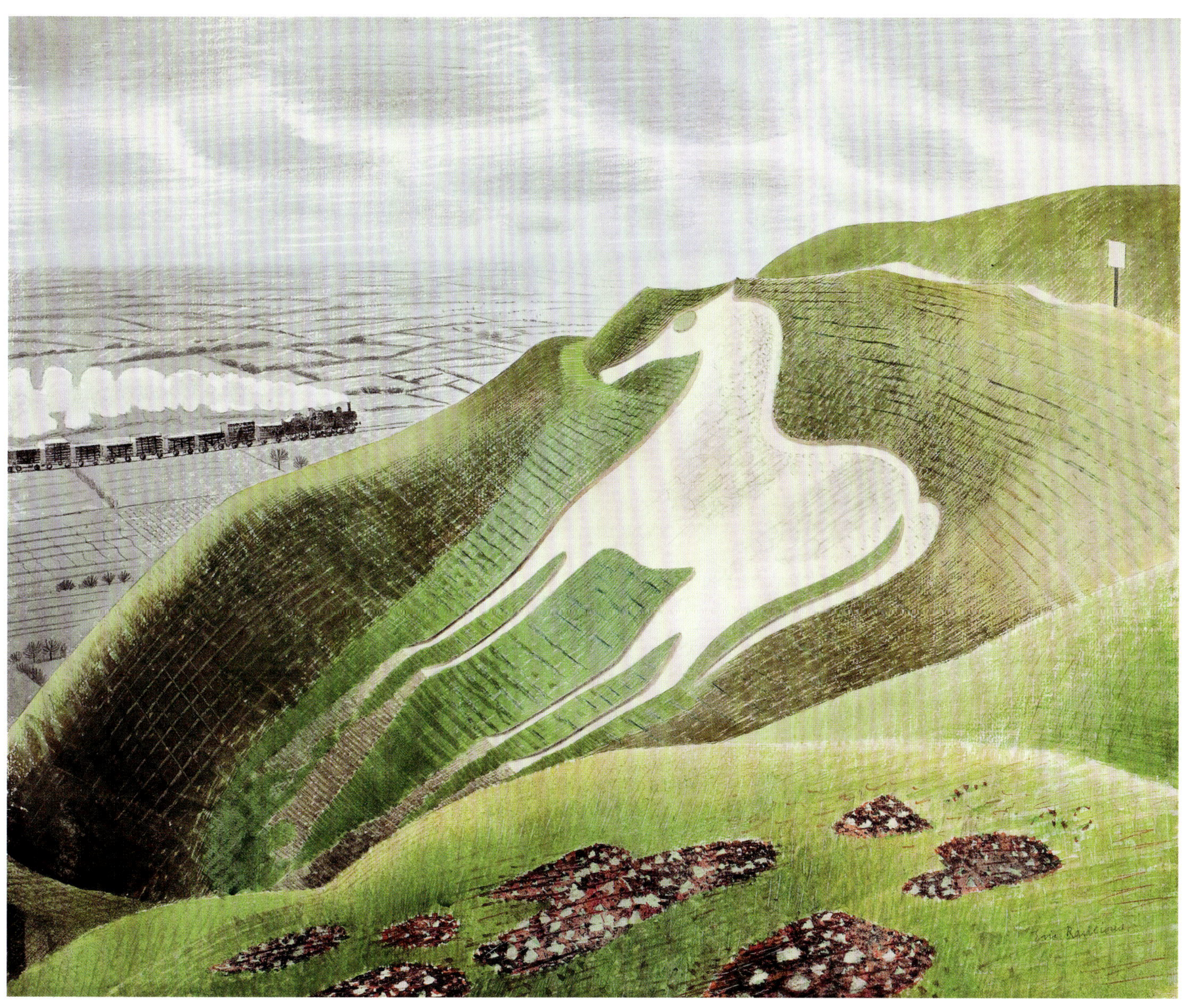

In the previous painting we saw a train from the viewpoint of the Westbury Horse; here the perspective is reversed, with the chalk figure framed by the window of a railway compartment. We take on the role of passenger, alone in the corner seat, looking up to see the horse appear on the hillside, as it does when a train approaches Westbury station.

In this instance, though, the eye is quickly drawn back into the empty compartment, to the huge number on the door. Yellow, shaded black, this massive numeral tells us our place. We're in third class, and the seat cushions, though exquisitely patterned with diamonds and stars, are starting to sag. These and the leather window strap, stretched out of shape by countless hands, indicate that this compartment is real and much used. Keep looking and more details appear, from the tab handles of the roller blinds to the patch of pale sunlight on the woodwork in the top left of the painting. The diagonally striped draught strips on either side of the door are both functional and decorative.

Is it significant that the compartment is third class? Ravilious worked easily alongside the printers at the Curwen Press and occasionally drew industrial workers and farm labourers, but he was equally comfortable among naval officers, or dining at the Café Royal. Rather than being a homage to the working man, the splendid '3' probably reflects his own economical travelling habits.

Until his appointment as a war artist nobody minded how Ravilious travelled, but in November 1940 the War Artists Advisory Committee found itself with a dilemma. With some artists claiming for first class travel and others for third, the WAAC stepped in. Ravilious, with a salary of £325 for six months' work, should travel third. As an officer holding the King's Commission, however, Captain Ravilious was not permitted to travel third class. 'I think,' wrote a committee member, 'we must let him go First.'

Ravilious travelled constantly by train, and it is fitting that he added to the canon of railway art this inimitable work. Where Turner's 'Rain, Steam and Speed' brilliantly conveys the violent drama of a transport revolution and Augustus Egg's 'Travelling Companions' the intimate experience of travel, Ravilious focuses on the magical space of the railway compartment itself, a man-made environment in which every detail is designed.

But this story has a twist. Restorers working on 'Train Landscape' recently discovered that the Westbury Horse had been glued over something else, and closer examination revealed the Wilmington Giant hidden behind it. It seems that, unusually for him, Ravilious made two paintings of a railway compartment with a Downland view, but was not happy with either. So Tirzah took the best parts of each and skilfully cut and pasted them together.

Train Landscape, 1939, watercolour, 44.4 x 54.6 cm, Aberdeen Art Gallery & Museums Collections.

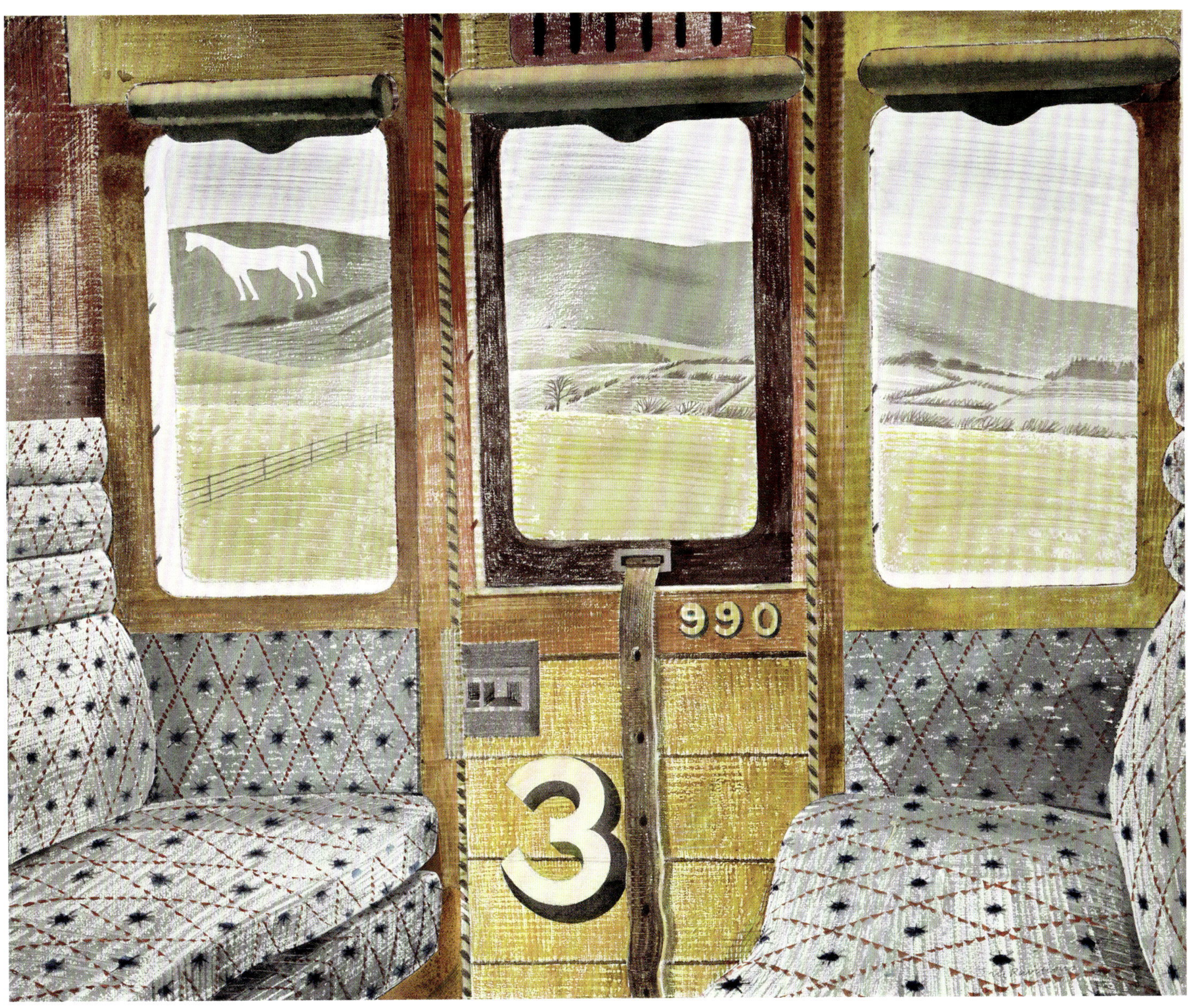

990
3

THE VALE OF THE WHITE HORSE

Of all the English chalk figures only the White Horse of Uffington, in the Berkshire Downs, can be reliably dated to prehistory. Evidence for the figure's venerability is plentiful, from written descriptions of the 11th century to recent optical dating, but its origins are uncertain. Local tradition insists that it is a dragon, not a horse, while legend connects the figure to King Alfred or Hengist, 5th-century leader of the Saxons. Carved in the Bronze Age, around 1000 BC, the White Horse was a tourist attraction as early as the 14th century, when the author of the *Tractatus de Mirabilibus Britanniae* ranked it second only to Stonehenge. Images of the figure appear on Iron Age coins and 20th-century album covers, while G. K. Chesterton celebrated the figure in verse and Thomas Hughes, author of *Tom Brown's Schooldays*, in his 1859 book, *The Scouring of the White Horse*.

If chalk figures are not routinely scoured they vanish. By tradition the task was performed during a fair held about every seven years within the Iron Age ramparts of neighbouring Uffington Castle; in his day Hughes witnessed stalls selling nuts, apples, gingerbread, toys, ribbons, and other trifles. There were musicians and acrobats, a publican's booth and a skittle alley, while contests included climbing a greasy pole, a pipe-smoking marathon and cheese rolling.

This took place in the Manger – the steep-sided, curiously shaped valley shown in this painting, which was also the scene for more macabre competitions: *Jackson's Oxford Journal* of 1780 records the game of riding down hill on a horse's jawbone.

This is an ancient site and an elemental scene, with rain falling from a luminous grey sky onto turf that seems to be stretched taut like skin over the underlying chalk. In the contours of the bristly grass slopes one might see a resemblance to Henry Moore's sculptures of the time, particularly 'Recumbent Figure', which was commissioned by Modernist architect Serge Chermayeff for the terrace of his new house at Halland in East Sussex. Ravilious and Chermayeff were friends, and the artist visited the celebrated house on 20 August 1939, two days before his son James was born. Reporting back to Diana Tuely he noted with typical insouciance that what he really enjoyed was playing boules in the garden. 'I simply loved this game,' he told her, 'and must and will get a set of boule balls one day.'

He was still extolling the virtues of this 'marvellous game' in November, when he suggested to Cecilia Dunbar Kilburn, co-owner of Dunbar Hay, that she sell boules sets. 'I played just before the war,' he told her, 'in Chermayeff's garden on a fine Sunday evening.'

The Vale of the White Horse, 1939, watercolour, 45.1 x 55.2 cm, Tate, London.

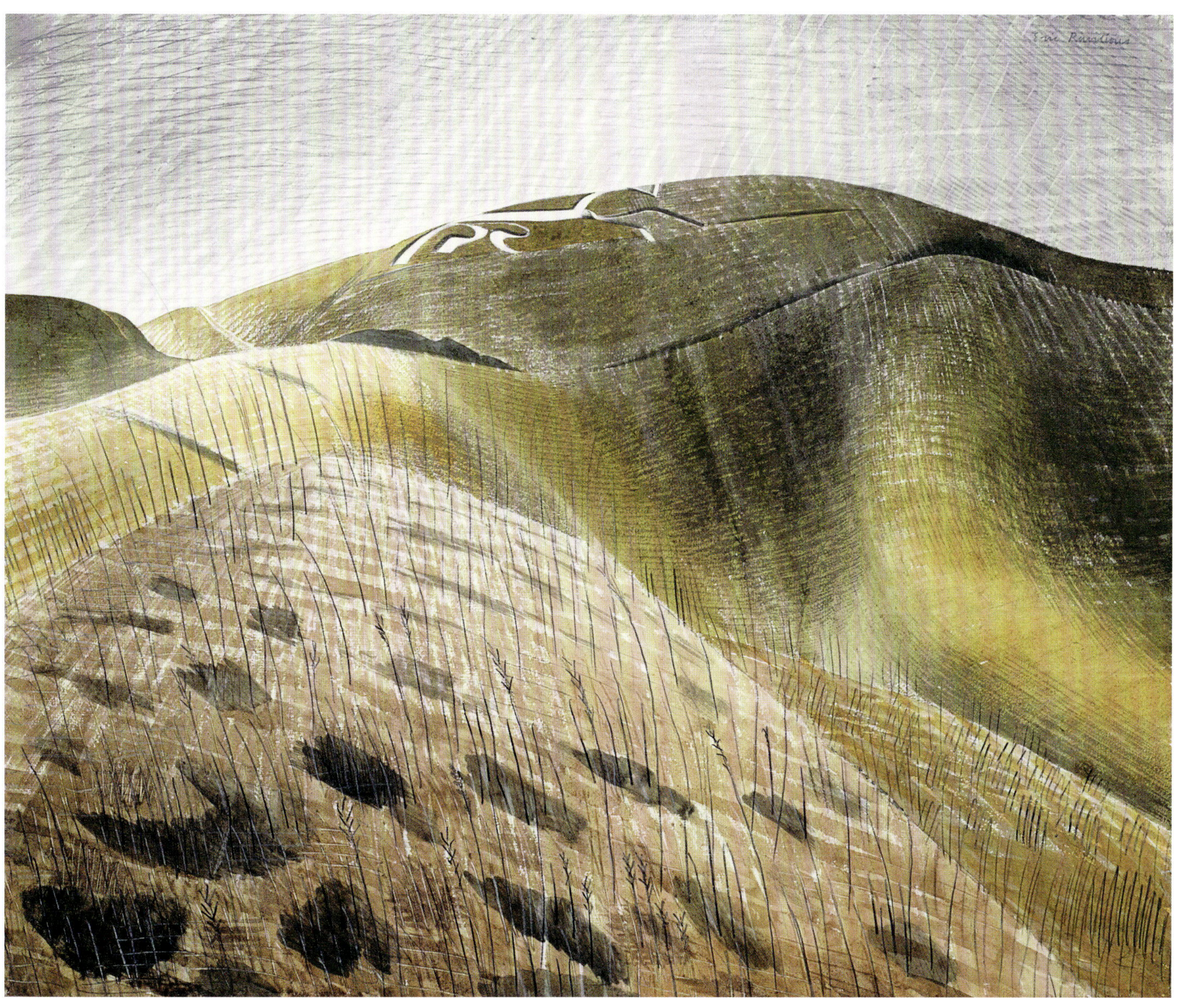

CHALK FIGURE NEAR WEYMOUTH

During the 1790s George III spent annual holidays in the Dorset port of Weymouth, establishing it as the first English seaside resort, and in 1808 this equestrian figure was carved into nearby Osmington Hill to celebrate his patronage. According to legend, he took offence at the positioning of the figure, which faces away from the town, and never returned, but in fact he visited Weymouth for the last time several years earlier. We tend to think of the white horse as an ancient and singularly English device, but it was also a heraldic symbol of the House of Hanover, the family of George I and his heirs. During the Georgian age the motif of a galloping horse was added to the Royal Coat of Arms, and some scholars believe that the Westbury Horse was carved to honour the German-born king.

By December 1939, when Ravilious took his whistlestop tour of Downland chalk figures, the two countries were at war and the risk of German air attacks was growing. Concerned that landmarks visible from the air could be used by enemy navigators, the War Office ordered landowners to conceal the distinctive white outlines of chalk figures with turf. There was every possibility, in those uncertain times, that they would remain so indefinitely. As for Ravilious, he would spend the rest of his career in the employ of the military establishment, devoting his skills to the war effort.

Assigned to the Admiralty, he painted coastal defences, submarines and ships, and in May 1940 sailed to Norway with the destroyer *HMS Highlander*. On his return he continued to paint naval installations, but was occasionally allocated a more unusual subject. On one occasion the War Artists Advisory Committee suggested he try a subject for which he seemed uniquely qualified, namely recording the concealment of white horses and other such images cut in the chalk. He was enthusiastic at first, but in the absence of photographs or sketches showing people laying turf over the chalk, he had to give up the idea.

But a second subject was also proposed. In a continuing effort to foil enemy navigators, the Ministry of Home Security had decided to conceal not only chalk figures but also the equally obvious white walls of Downland road and railway cuttings. Given the scale of the operation, the men from the Ministry reasoned, the best way to do this was by spraying black ink from fire engines. One can only imagine the chaos when the local Home Guard manned the hoses; soon afterwards Ravilious received a terse note from the WAAC. 'The spraying of chalk cuttings with ink from fire engines,' it explained, 'was an experiment that was not repeated.'

Chalk Figure near Weymouth, 1939, watercolour, 44.3 x 55.4 cm, National Gallery of Canada, Ottawa.

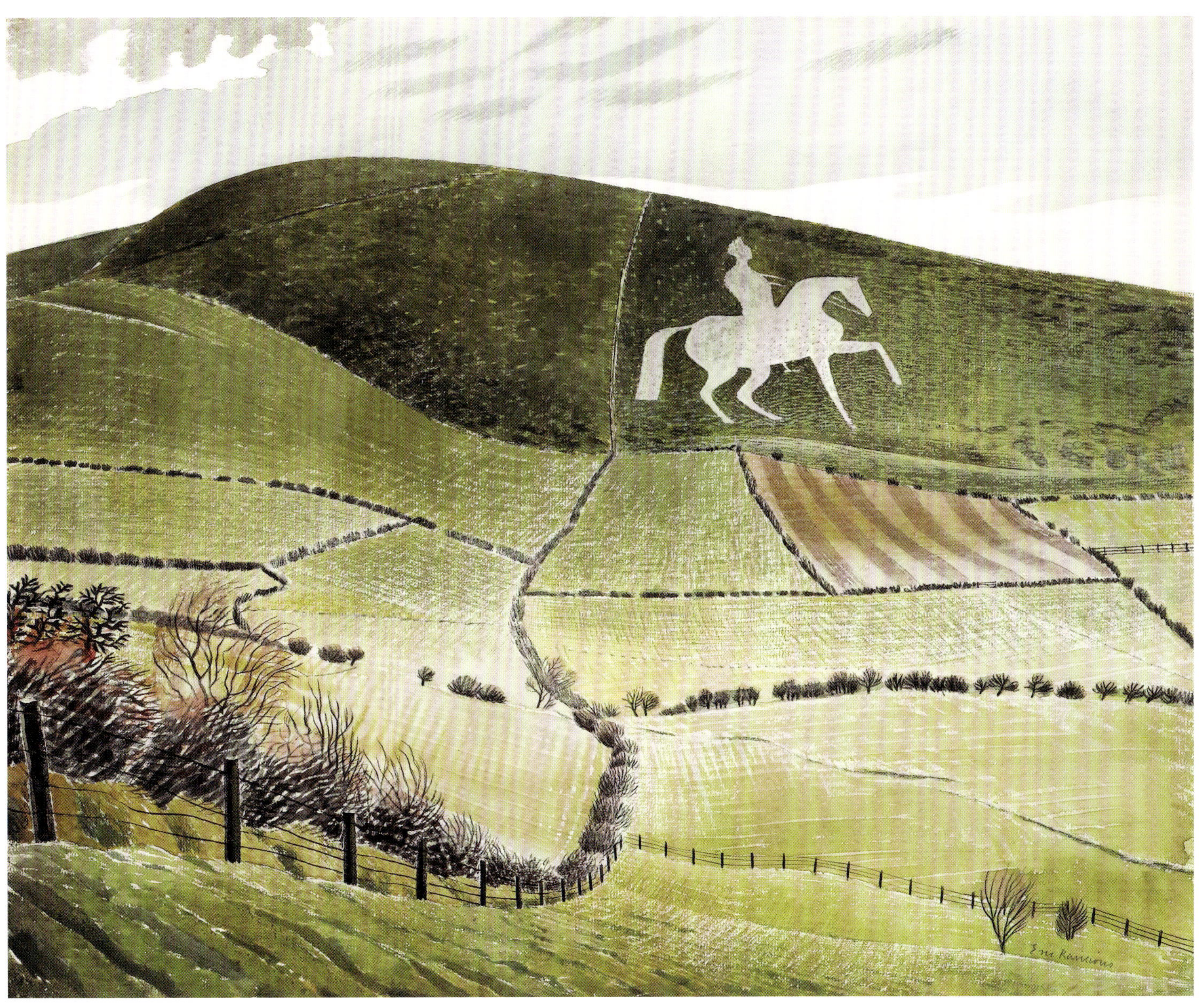

Its well-known outline already covered in turf to confound hostile pilots and navigators, the Cerne Abbas Giant is here transformed from white chalk figure to martial Green Man, body striped like a pagan chieftain, arms brandishing a knotted club. Cloud swirls over the scene, obscuring the hills as the green turf conceals the chalk, while broken earth and barbed wire dominate the foreground. Ravilious had included barbed-wire fences in several watercolours of the Downs, but here the crooked posts and twisting wire recall the work of his friend John Nash, whose paintings of trench warfare helped to define our collective memory of World War I.

Ravilious wrote to Nash in July 1939, asking his advice on whether or not to join the Artists' Rifles, the regiment in which his colleague had served between 1916 and 1918. Although by reputation a somewhat distant character, Ravilious was determined to serve in whatever capacity he could. Nash advised him not to rush in, suggesting that his talents would be put to better use elsewhere, which proved to be the case. In his official role of war artist he returned to a more detached style, leaving this as a work of unusual intimacy and menace.

Seeing this brooding picture, one might wonder at the artist's state of mind, yet he wrote from the New Inn at Cerne Abbas in his usual bright tone, describing the giant as a marvellous figure, and asking Tirzah if he should buy more postcards – he had already acquired forty.

The postcard, which shows an aerial photograph of the giant taken by London-based company Aero Pictorial, was sold at the News Agency in Cerne Abbas to metropolitan tourists who braved the Dorset hills in their motor cars to witness this infamous curiosity. The figure was first mentioned in writing in 1694, and the absence of earlier references to such a remarkable landmark suggests that it was carved not long before. Eighteenth-century antiquarian William Stukeley saw in the carving a representation of the classical hero Heracles, while Dorset folklore has long associated the giant with fertility. It inspired Ravilious to get out and paint, in spite of uncertain wintry weather and a touch of rheumatism in his shoulders.

'This morning,' he wrote to Tirzah, 'in my excitement at the burst of sunshine I took a 5 bar gate a bit close and all but cut my breeches in two on a prong of barbed wire. You never saw such a tear; but the girl here (one of the girls, there are great numbers here) mended it for me.'

It is a delightful image: the artist, full of enthusiasm for his work, springing over a fence. Hard times lay ahead but Ravilious faced them cheerfully, making the most of the winter sunlight.

The Cerne Abbas Giant, 1939, watercolour, 44.5 x 54.6 cm, private collection.

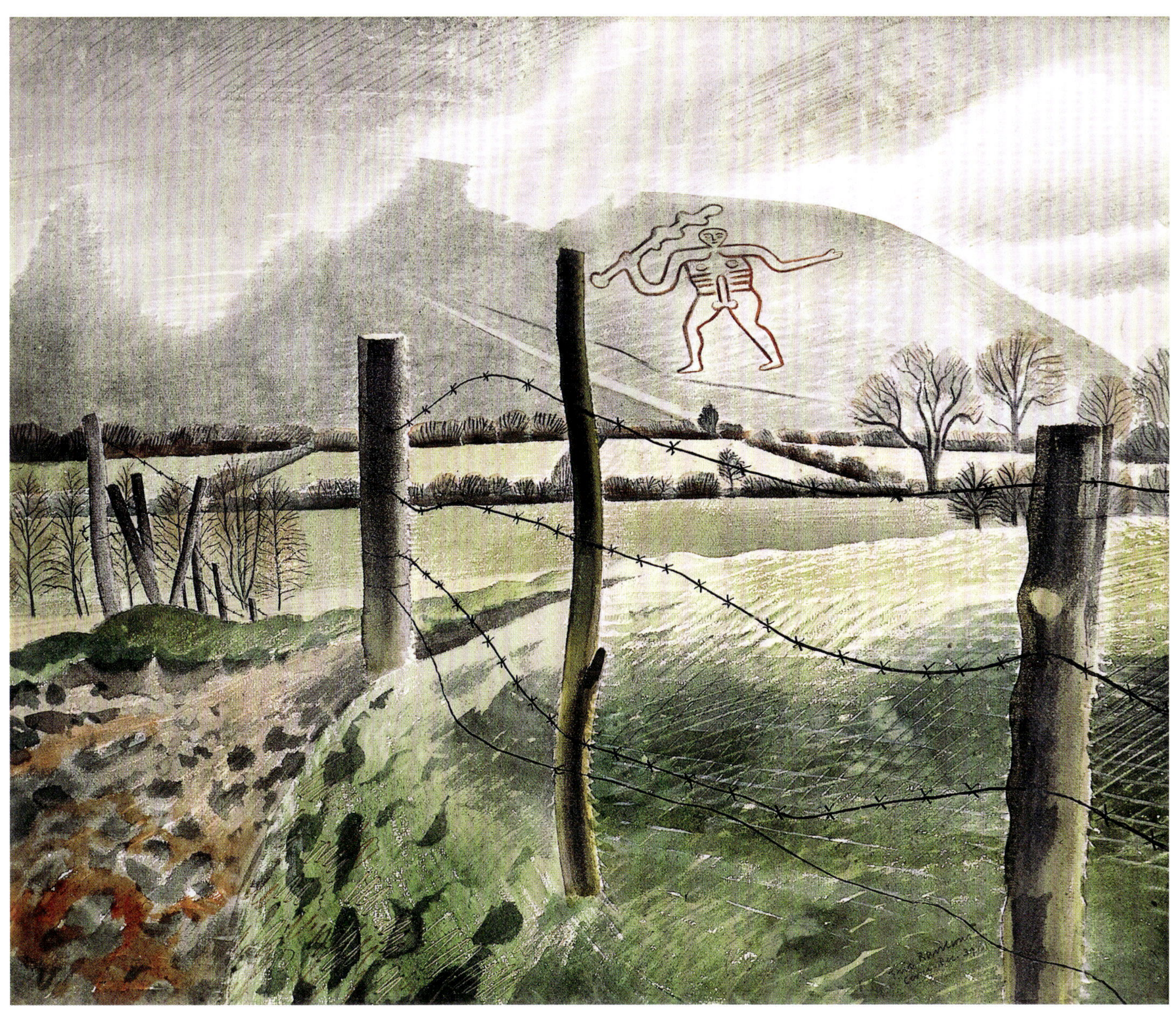

First published in December 2009 by
The Mainstone Press, Vivian Road, London E3 5RF
www.themainstonepress.com

ISBN 978-0-9552777-3-3

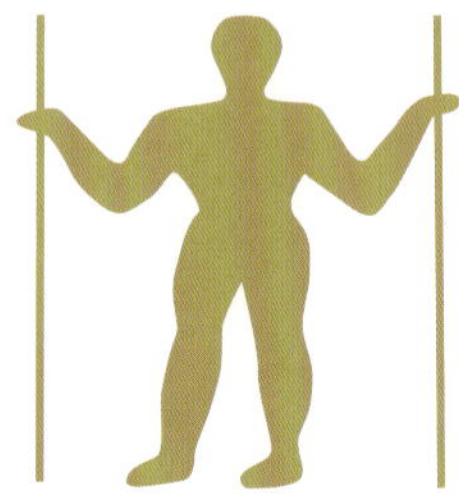

Text © James Russell & The Mainstone Press
Edited by Tim Mainstone / Design by Webb & Webb
Printed by Graphicom, Italy

We are indebted to Anne Ullmann, the artist's daughter, and to Christopher
Whittick. Quotations from the correspondence of Eric Ravilious are mostly
taken from their book *Eric Ravilious: Landscape, Letters and Design*. We would
like to thank Simon Lawrence of the Fleece Press for his invaluable help,
and Andrew Lusted, Jim Piper and Robin Ravilious for their assistance in
researching the book. Lastly, many thanks to Dayna Stevens and
Sally Randall for their encouragement and support.

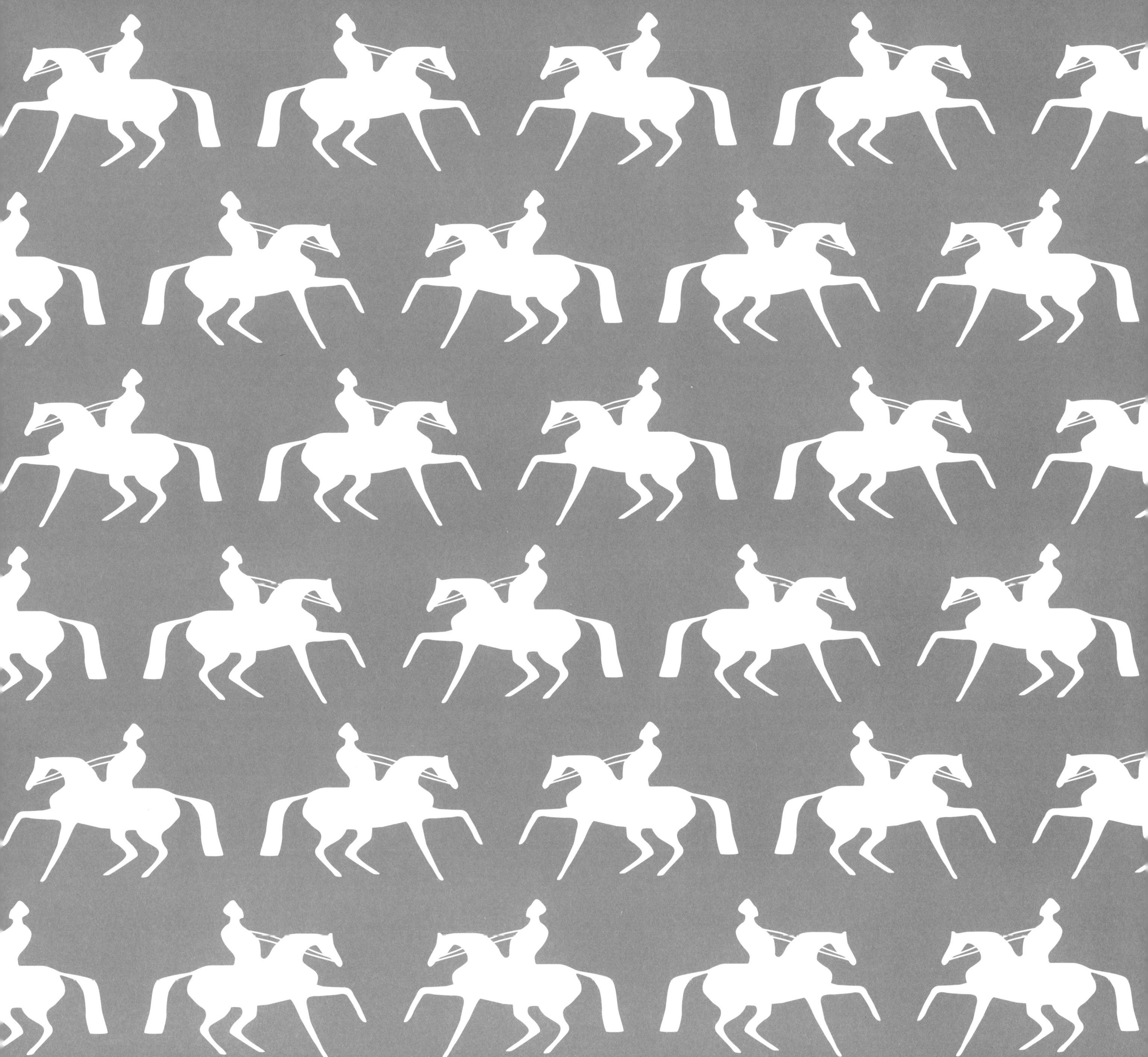

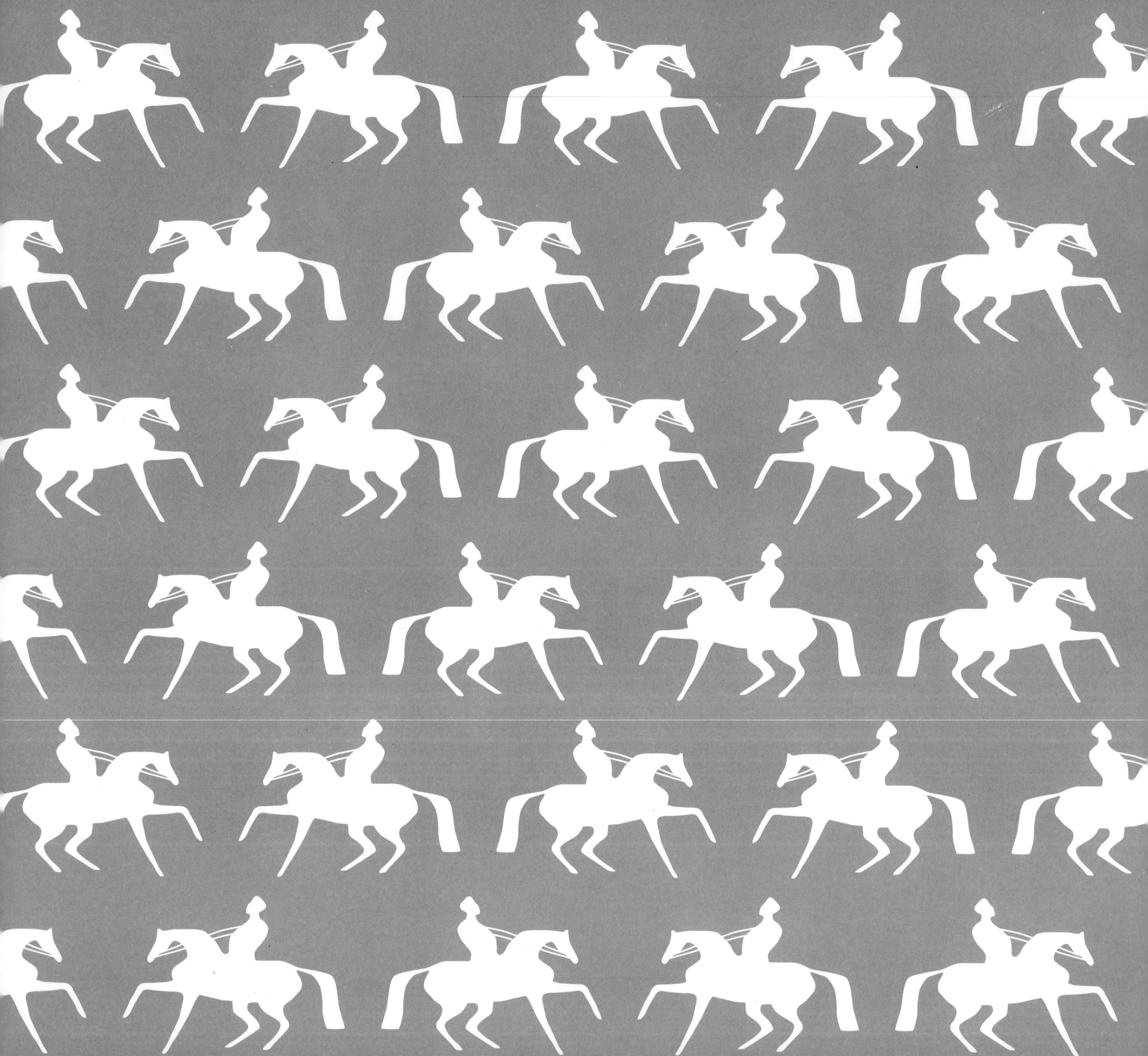